Soups & Stews

Table of
Contents

beef 'n' Pork

Spicy Pork Stew with Veggies

      1 teaspoon olive oil
 1½ pounds boneless pork loin, trimmed and
          cut into ½-inch cubes
      1 acorn squash, peeled and cut into ½-inch cubes
      1 can (about 14 ounces) diced tomatoes
      1 can (about 14 ounces) chicken broth
      2 red bell peppers, cut into ½-inch pieces
      1 onion, chopped
      1 container (8 ounces) sliced mushrooms
    ½ teaspoon red pepper flakes
    ½ teaspoon black pepper
    ½ teaspoon dried thyme
      Fresh oregano (optional)

1. Heat oil in Dutch oven over medium-high heat. Add half of pork; cook 5 minutes or until browned, stirring occasionally. Repeat with remaining pork.

2. Stir in squash, tomatoes, broth, bell peppers, onion, mushrooms, red pepper flakes, black pepper and thyme; bring to a boil over high heat. Reduce heat to medium-low. Cover and simmer 1 hour or until pork is tender. Garnish with oregano.   *Makes 8 servings*

Pasta Meatball Soup

  10 **ounces ground beef**
   5 **tablespoons uncooked acini di pepe pasta,★ divided**
 ¼ **cup fresh bread crumbs**
  1 **egg**
  2 **tablespoons finely chopped fresh parsley, divided**
  1 **teaspoon dried basil, divided**
  1 **clove garlic, minced**
 ¼ **teaspoon salt**
 ⅛ **teaspoon black pepper**
  2 **cans (about 14 ounces each) beef broth**
  1 **can (about 8 ounces) tomato sauce**
 ⅓ **cup chopped onion**

★*Acini di pepe is tiny rice-shaped pasta. Orzo or pastina can be substituted.*

1. Combine beef, 2 tablespoons pasta, bread crumbs, egg, 1 tablespoon parsley, ½ teaspoon basil, garlic, salt and pepper in medium bowl. Shape into 28 to 30 (1-inch) meatballs.

2. Combine broth, tomato sauce, onion and remaining ½ teaspoon basil in large bowl; bring to a boil in large saucepan over medium-high heat. Carefully add meatballs to broth mixture. Reduce heat to medium-low. Cover and simmer 20 minutes.

3. Add remaining 3 tablespoons pasta; cook 10 minutes or until tender. Garnish with remaining 1 tablespoon parsley.   *Makes 4 servings*

Beefy Broccoli & Cheese Soup

¼ **pound ground beef**
2 **cups beef broth**
1 **package (10 ounces) frozen chopped broccoli, thawed**
¼ **cup chopped onion**
1 **cup milk**
2 **tablespoons all-purpose flour**
1 **cup (4 ounces) shredded sharp Cheddar cheese**
1½ **teaspoons chopped fresh oregano** *or* ½ **teaspoon dried oregano**
   Salt and black pepper
   Hot pepper sauce

1. Brown beef 6 to 8 minutes in large nonstick skillet over medium-high heat, stirring to break up meat. Drain fat.

2. Bring broth to a boil in medium saucepan over high heat. Add broccoli and onion; cook 5 minutes or until broccoli is tender. Stir milk into flour in small bowl until smooth. Stir milk mixture and ground beef into saucepan; cook and stir until mixture is thickened and heated through.

3. Add cheese and oregano; stir until cheese is melted. Season with salt, black pepper and hot pepper sauce.   *Makes 4 servings*

tip: The wonderful flavor in herbs comes from aromatic essential oils that are released by chopping and/or heating. When herbs are dried these oils become concentrated, so when substituting dried herbs for fresh herbs, use about one third as much.

Jerk Pork and Sweet Potato Stew

2 tablespoons all-purpose flour
¼ teaspoon salt
¼ teaspoon black pepper
1¼ pounds pork shoulder, cut into bite-size pieces
2 tablespoons vegetable oil
1 sweet potato, peeled and diced
1 cup corn
4 tablespoons minced green onions, divided
1 clove garlic, minced
½ medium Scotch bonnet chile or jalapeño pepper,★
    seeded and minced
⅛ teaspoon ground allspice
1 cup chicken broth
1 tablespoon lime juice
2 cups hot cooked rice

★*Scotch bonnet chiles and jalapeño peppers can sting and irritate the skin, so wear rubber gloves when handling and do not touch your eyes.*

Slow Cooker Directions

1. Combine flour, salt and black pepper in large resealable food storage bag. Add pork; shake well to coat. Heat oil in large skillet over medium heat. Working in batches, brown pork on all sides. Transfer to 4- or 5-quart slow cooker.

2. Add sweet potato, corn, 2 tablespoons green onions, garlic, chile and allspice. Stir in broth. Cover; cook on LOW 5 to 6 hours.

3. Stir in lime juice and remaining 2 tablespoons green onions. Serve with rice.

Makes 4 servings

Prep Time: 15 minutes • **Cook Time:** 5 to 6 hours

Beef Barley Soup

Nonstick cooking spray
¾ pound boneless beef top round steak, trimmed and
    cut into ½-inch pieces
3 cans (about 14 ounces each) beef broth
1 can (about 14 ounces) diced tomatoes
1 potato, unpeeled and cut into ½-inch cubes
1 cup chopped onion
1 cup sliced carrots
½ cup uncooked pearl barley
1 tablespoon cider vinegar
2 teaspoons caraway seeds
2 teaspoons dried marjoram
2 teaspoons dried thyme
½ teaspoon salt
½ teaspoon black pepper
1½ cups sliced green beans

1. Spray large saucepan with cooking spray; heat over medium heat. Add beef; cook and stir until browned on all sides.

2. Stir in broth, tomatoes, potato, onion, carrots, barley, vinegar, caraway seeds, marjoram, thyme, salt and pepper; bring to a boil over high heat. Reduce heat to low. Cover and simmer 2 hours or until beef is fork-tender. Add green beans during last 30 minutes of cooking. *Makes 4 servings*

New Mexican Green Chile Pork Stew

1½ pounds boneless pork shoulder, cut into 1-inch cubes
2 baking potatoes or sweet potatoes, peeled and
   cut into large chunks
1 cup chopped onion
1 cup frozen corn
1 can (4 ounces) diced green chiles
1 jar (16 ounces) salsa verde (green salsa)
2 teaspoons sugar
2 teaspoons ground cumin or chili powder
1 teaspoon dried oregano
   Hot cooked rice
¼ cup chopped fresh cilantro (optional)

Slow Cooker Directions

1. Place pork, potatoes, onion, corn and chiles in slow cooker. Combine salsa, sugar, cumin and oregano in small bowl. Pour over pork and vegetables; stir gently to mix.

2. Cover; cook on LOW 6 to 8 hours or on HIGH 4 to 5 hours. Serve stew with rice. Garnish with cilantro. *Makes 6 servings*

Prep Time: 15 minutes • **Cook Time:** 6 to 8 hours (LOW) or 4 to 5 hours (HIGH)

Golden Harvest Pork Stew

1 pound boneless pork cutlets, cut into 1-inch pieces
2 tablespoons all-purpose flour, divided
1 tablespoon vegetable oil
2 Yukon Gold potatoes, unpeeled and cut into 1-inch cubes
1 sweet potato, peeled and cut into 1-inch cubes
1 cup chopped carrots
1 ear corn, broken into 4 pieces *or* ½ cup corn kernels
½ cup chicken broth
1 jalapeño pepper,★ seeded and finely chopped
1 clove garlic, minced
1 teaspoon salt
¼ teaspoon black pepper
¼ teaspoon dried thyme

★Jalapeño peppers can sting and irritate the skin, so wear rubber gloves when handling peppers and do not touch your eyes.

Slow Cooker Directions

1. Toss pork with 1 tablespoon flour. Heat oil in large nonstick skillet over medium-high heat; brown pork on all sides. Transfer to slow cooker. Add potatoes, sweet potato, carrots, corn, broth, jalapeño, garlic, salt, black pepper and thyme to slow cooker.

2. Cover; cook on LOW 5 to 6 hours.

3. *Turn slow cooker to HIGH.* Whisk remaining 1 tablespoon flour into ¼ cup cooking liquid in small bowl until smooth. Stir into stew. Cook, uncovered, 10 minutes or until thickened. *Makes 4 servings*

Prep Time: 15 minutes • **Cook Time:** 5 to 6 hours

Country Sausage and Bean Soup

2 cans (about 14 ounces each) chicken broth
1½ cups hot water
1 cup dried black beans, rinsed and sorted
1 cup chopped yellow onion
2 bay leaves
⅛ teaspoon ground red pepper
6 ounces bulk pork sausage
1 cup chopped tomato
1 tablespoon chili powder
1 tablespoon Worcestershire sauce
2 teaspoons olive oil
1½ teaspoons ground cumin
½ teaspoon salt
¼ cup chopped fresh cilantro

Slow Cooker Directions

1. Combine broth, water, beans, onion, bay leaves and red pepper in slow cooker. Cover; cook on LOW 8 hours or on HIGH 4 hours.

2. Brown sausage 6 to 8 minutes in medium saucepan over medium heat, stirring to break up meat. Drain fat. Add sausage, tomato, chili powder, Worcestershire sauce, oil, cumin and salt to slow cooker. *Turn slow cooker to HIGH.*

3. Cover; cook 15 minutes. Remove and discard bay leaves. Sprinkle with cilantro. *Makes 9 servings*

Kansas City Steak Soup

½ **pound ground beef**
3 **cups frozen mixed vegetables**
2 **cups water**
1 **can (about 14 ounces) stewed tomatoes**
1 **cup chopped onion**
1 **cup sliced celery**
1 **beef bouillon cube**
½ **to 1 teaspoon black pepper**
1 **can (about 14 ounces) beef broth**
½ **cup all-purpose flour**

1. Brown beef 6 to 8 minutes in large saucepan over medium-high heat, stirring to break up meat. Drain fat.

2. Add mixed vegetables, water, tomatoes, onion, celery, bouillon cube and pepper to saucepan; bring to a boil.

3. Stir broth into flour in small bowl until smooth. Add to beef mixture; stir until blended. Bring to a boil. Reduce heat to medium-low. Cover and simmer 15 minutes, stirring frequently.   *Makes 6 servings*

tip: If time allows, simmer this soup an additional 30 minutes to further blend the flavors.

Mushroom-Beef Stew

1 pound beef stew meat
1 can (10¾ ounces) condensed cream of mushroom soup, undiluted
2 cans (4 ounces each) sliced mushrooms, drained
1 package (1 ounce) dry onion soup mix
   Hot cooked noodles

Slow Cooker Directions

1. Combine beef, condensed soup, mushrooms and soup mix in slow cooker.

2. Cover; cook on LOW 8 to 10 hours. Serve over noodles.

Makes 4 servings

Long Soup

1½ tablespoons vegetable oil
  8 ounces boneless lean pork, cut into thin strips
  ¼ small head cabbage, shredded
  6 cups chicken broth
  2 tablespoons soy sauce
  ½ teaspoon minced fresh ginger
  8 green onions, cut diagonally into ½-inch slices
  4 ounces uncooked Chinese-style thin egg noodles

1. Heat oil in wok or large skillet over medium-high heat. Add pork and cabbage; stir-fry 5 minutes or until pork is barely pink in center.

2. Add broth, soy sauce and ginger; bring to a boil. Reduce heat to low. Simmer 10 minutes, stirring occasionally.

3. Stir in green onions. Add noodles; cook 2 to 4 minutes or until tender.

Makes 4 servings

Swiss Steak Stew

2 to 3 boneless beef top sirloin steaks (about 4 pounds)
2 cans (about 14 ounces each) diced tomatoes
2 green bell peppers, cut into $\frac{1}{2}$-inch strips
2 onions, chopped
1 tablespoon seasoned salt
1 teaspoon black pepper

Slow Cooker Directions

1. Cut each steak into 3 to 4 pieces; place in slow cooker. Add tomatoes, bell peppers and onions. Sprinkle with seasoned salt and black pepper.

2. Cover; cook on LOW 8 hours.   *Makes 10 servings*

Beef Fajita Soup

1 pound beef stew meat
1 can (15 ounces) pinto beans, rinsed and drained
1 can (15 ounces) black beans, rinsed and drained
1 can (about 14 ounces) diced tomatoes with roasted garlic
1 can (about 14 ounces) beef broth
1 green bell pepper, thinly sliced
1 red bell pepper, thinly sliced
1 onion, thinly sliced
1$\frac{1}{2}$ cups water
2 teaspoons ground cumin
1 teaspoon seasoned salt
1 teaspoon black pepper
    Toppings: sour cream, shredded Monterey Jack or Cheddar cheese
        and/or chopped olives

Slow Cooker Directions

1. Combine beef, beans, tomatoes, broth, bell peppers, onion, water, cumin, salt and black pepper in slow cooker.

2. Cover; cook on LOW 8 hours. Serve with toppings.   *Makes 8 servings*

Slow Cooker Beef Barley Soup

1½ pounds beef stew meat, cut in ½-inch pieces
1 teaspoon salt
½ teaspoon black pepper
5 cups beef broth
2 carrots, quartered lengthwise and cut into ½-inch pieces
1 cup chopped onion
1 package (8 ounces) sliced mushrooms
1 leek, halved and thinly sliced
2 tablespoons Worcestershire sauce
1 teaspoon soy sauce
1 bay leaf
1 cup frozen mixed vegetables, thawed
¾ cup barley

Slow Cooker Directions

1. Season beef with salt and pepper; place in slow cooker. Add broth, carrots, onion, mushrooms, leek, Worcestershire sauce, soy sauce and bay leaf.

2. Cover; cook on LOW 6 hours.

3. Stir in mixed vegetables and barley. Cover; cook on LOW 1 to 2 hours or until beef is fork-tender. Remove and discard bay leaf before serving.

Makes 8 servings

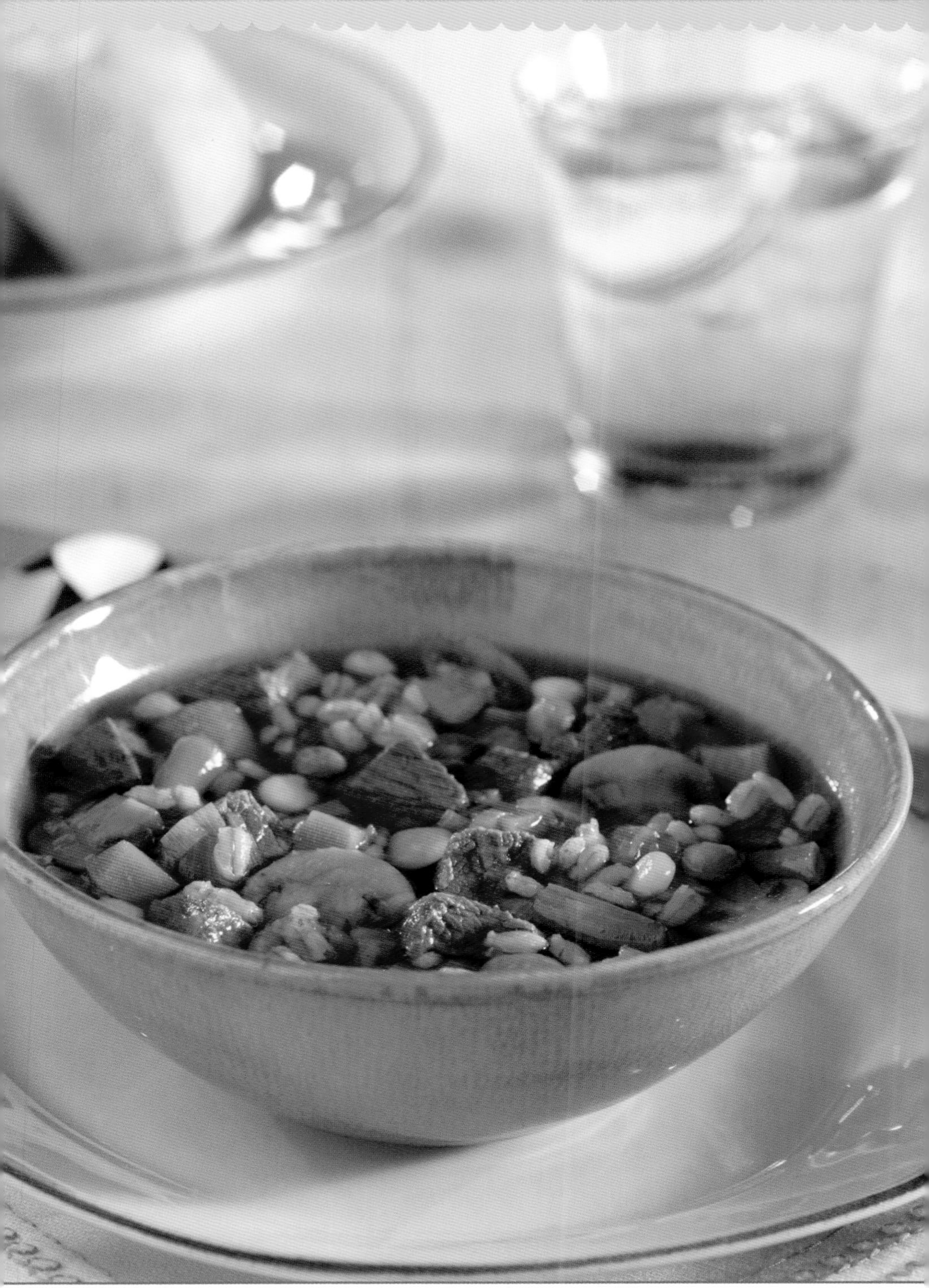

Italian Sausage Soup

Sausage Meatballs

   1 pound mild Italian sausage, casings removed
   ½ cup plain dry bread crumbs
   ¼ cup grated Parmesan cheese
   ¼ cup milk
   1 egg
   ½ teaspoon dried basil
   ½ teaspoon black pepper
   ¼ teaspoon garlic salt

Soup

   4 cups chicken broth
   1 tablespoon tomato paste
   1 clove garlic, minced
   ¼ teaspoon red pepper flakes
   ½ cup uncooked mini shell pasta★
   1 package (10 ounces) baby spinach
   Additional grated Parmesan cheese (optional)

★Or use other mini pasta, such as ditalini (mini tubes) or farfallini (mini bow ties).

Slow Cooker Directions

1. Combine sausage, bread crumbs, ¼ cup cheese, milk, egg, basil, black pepper and garlic salt in large bowl. Shape into marble-size balls.

2. Combine broth, tomato paste, garlic and red pepper flakes in slow cooker. Add meatballs.

3. Cover; cook on LOW 5 to 6 hours.

4. Stir in pasta; cook, covered, on LOW 30 minutes or until pasta is tender. Stir in spinach until wilted. Sprinkle with additional cheese, if desired.

Makes 4 to 6 servings

quick 'n'
Easy

Quick and Zesty Vegetable Soup

 1 pound lean ground beef
 ½ cup chopped onion
    Salt and pepper
 2 cans (14½ ounces each) **DEL MONTE**® Italian Recipe
    Stewed Tomatoes
 2 cans (14 ounces each) beef broth
 1 can (14½ ounces) **DEL MONTE**® Mixed Vegetables
 ½ cup uncooked medium egg noodles
 ½ teaspoon dried oregano

1. Brown meat with onion in large pot. Cook until onion is tender; drain. Season to taste with salt and pepper.

2. Stir in remaining ingredients. Bring to boil; reduce heat.

3. Cover and simmer 15 minutes or until noodles are tender.

Makes 8 servings

Prep Time: 5 minutes • **Cook Time:** 15 minutes

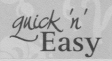
All-in-One Burger Stew

1 pound ground beef
2 cups frozen Italian-style vegetables
1 can (about 14 ounces) diced tomatoes with basil and garlic
1 can (about 14 ounces) beef broth
2½ cups uncooked medium egg noodles
Salt and black pepper
Fresh chopped parsley (optional)

1. Brown beef 6 to 8 minutes in Dutch oven over medium-high heat, stirring to break up meat. Drain fat.

2. Add vegetables, tomatoes and broth; bring to a boil over high heat. Add noodles; reduce heat to medium.

3. Cover; cook 12 to 15 minutes or until noodles and vegetables are tender. Season with salt and pepper. Garnish with parsley.   *Makes 6 servings*

Prep and Cook Time: 25 minutes

Wild Rice Soup

½ cup dried lentils, rinsed and sorted
3 cups water
1 package (6 ounces) long grain and wild rice blend
1 can (about 14 ounces) vegetable broth
1 package (10 ounces) frozen mixed vegetables
1 cup milk
2 slices (1 ounce each) American cheese, cut into pieces

1. Place lentils in small saucepan; cover with water. Bring to a boil. Reduce heat to low. Cover and simmer 5 minutes. Let stand, covered, 1 hour. Drain and rinse lentils.

2. Cook rice according to package directions in medium saucepan. Add lentils, broth, vegetables, milk and cheese; bring to a boil. Reduce heat to low. Simmer, uncovered, 20 minutes.   *Makes 6 servings*

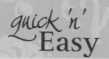

Chicken Tortellini Soup

6 cups chicken broth
1 package (9 ounces) refrigerated cheese and spinach tortellini
1 package (about 6 ounces) refrigerated fully cooked chicken breast strips
2 cups baby spinach
4 to 6 tablespoons grated Parmesan cheese
1 tablespoon chopped fresh chives *or* 2 tablespoons sliced green onion

1. Bring broth to a boil in large saucepan over high heat; add tortellini. Reduce heat to medium-low. Cook 5 minutes.

2. Cut chicken into bite-size pieces. Stir chicken and spinach into saucepan. Reduce heat to low. Cook 3 minutes or until chicken is heated through. Sprinkle with Parmesan and chives.   *Makes 4 servings*

Beef Stew in Bread Bowls

2 packages TYSON® Heat 'N Eat Beef Tips in Gravy,★ 17 ounces
1 can reduced-sodium vegetable soup
1 can potato soup
2 tablespoons rosemary
4 large sized rolls, hard and crusty

★*Look for TYSON® Heat 'N Eat Beef Tips in Gravy in your supermarket's refrigerated meat case.*

1. Preheat oven to 325°F. Empty contents of TYSON® Beef Tips in Gravy into a conventional oven-safe bowl.

2. Strain liquid from the reduced-sodium vegetable and potato soup cans and discard liquid. Empty all of the vegetables and potatoes into the conventional oven-safe bowl and mix well. Sprinkle rosemary over the stew mixture and heat for 20 minutes or until contents are hot and steaming.

3. Using sharp knife, cut in a circular motion around the tops of the crusty rolls; removing the tops. Pull bread center out to form bowls for the stew and place the pulled bread pieces to the side.

4. Spoon the hot stew into the bread bowls and use the tops and pulled bread pieces to dip into the stew.   *Makes 4 servings*

Prep Time: 5 minutes • **Cook Time:** 20 minutes • **Total Time:** 25 minutes

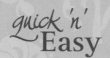

Quick & Easy Ravioli Soup

½ **pound mild Italian sausage, casings removed**
½ **cup chopped onion**
 1 **clove garlic, minced**
 2 **cans (about 14 ounces each) chicken broth**
 2 **cups water**
 1 **package (9 ounces) frozen mini cheese-filled ravioli**
 1 **can (about 15 ounces) chickpeas, rinsed and drained**
 1 **can (about 14 ounces) diced tomatoes with green chiles**
¾ **teaspoon dried oregano**
½ **teaspoon black pepper**
 1 **cup baby spinach**
   Grated Parmesan cheese

1. Brown sausage, onion and garlic 5 minutes in Dutch oven over medium heat, stirring to break up meat. Drain fat. Remove sausage mixture to large bowl.

2. Add broth and water to Dutch oven; bring to a boil over medium-high heat. Add ravioli; cook 4 to 5 minutes or until tender. Stir in sausage mixture, chickpeas, tomatoes, oregano and pepper; cook and stir 5 minutes or until heated through. Stir in spinach; cook 1 minute or until wilted. Sprinkle evenly with cheese. *Makes 8 servings*

Italian Fish Soup

 1 **cup meatless pasta sauce**
¾ **cup *each* chicken broth and water**
 1 **teaspoon Italian seasoning**
¾ **cup uncooked small pasta shells**
 4 **ounces (1 inch thick) fresh halibut, skinned and cut into 1-inch pieces**
1½ **cups frozen vegetable blend, such as broccoli, carrots and**
     water chestnuts

1. Combine pasta sauce, broth, water and Italian seasoning in medium saucepan; bring to a boil. Stir in pasta; return to a boil. Reduce heat to medium. Cover and simmer 5 minutes.

2. Stir in fish and vegetables; return to a boil. Reduce heat to medium. Cover and simmer 4 to 5 minutes or until fish flakes easily when tested with fork and pasta is tender. *Makes 2 servings*

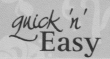

Broccoli, Cheese and Rice Soup

2 cups **MINUTE**® White or Brown Rice, uncooked
1 package (10 ounces) frozen chopped broccoli, thawed
1 can (10¾ ounces) reduced-fat cream of mushroom soup
3 cups low-fat milk
1 pound low-fat processed cheese, cubed
    Shredded cheese (optional)

Prepare rice according to package directions.

Combine broccoli, soup and milk in medium saucepan. Bring to a simmer over medium heat.

Add cheese and stir until melted. Remove from heat and stir in rice. Top with shredded cheese, if desired. *Makes 6 servings*

Quick & Easy Meatball Soup

1 package (15 to 18 ounces) frozen Italian sausage meatballs
    without sauce
2 cans (about 14 ounces each) Italian-style stewed tomatoes
2 cans (about 14 ounces each) beef broth
1 can (about 14 ounces) mixed vegetables
½ cup uncooked rotini pasta or small macaroni
½ teaspoon dried oregano

1. Thaw meatballs in microwave according to package directions.

2. Place tomatoes, broth, vegetables, pasta and oregano in large saucepan. Add meatballs; bring to a boil. Reduce heat to medium-low. Cover and simmer 15 minutes or until pasta is tender. *Makes 4 to 6 servings*

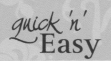

Minestrone Soup

4 cups water
¾ cup small shell pasta
2 cans (about 14 ounces each) vegetable broth
1 can (about 28 ounces) crushed tomatoes
1 can (15 ounces) white beans, rinsed and drained
1 package (16 ounces) frozen vegetable medley, such as broccoli, green
      beans, carrots and red peppers
4 to 6 teaspoons prepared pesto

1. Bring water to a boil in large saucepan over high heat. Stir in pasta; cook 8 to 10 minutes or until tender. Drain.

2. Meanwhile, combine broth, tomatoes and beans in Dutch oven. Cover and bring to a boil over high heat. Reduce heat to medium-low. Simmer 3 to 5 minutes.

3. Add vegetables to Dutch oven; return to a boil over high heat. Stir in pasta; simmer until vegetables and pasta are heated through. Spoon about 1 teaspoon pesto in center of each serving.   *Makes 4 to 6 servings*

Prep and Cook Time: 20 minutes

Veg•All® Black Bean Soup

1 package (14 ounces) smoked sausage, cut into ½-inch slices
2 cans (15 ounces each) VEG•ALL® Original Mixed Vegetables
2 cans (15 ounces each) black beans with spices, drained and rinsed
2 cans (14½ ounces) chicken broth

In large soup kettle, lightly brown sausage. Add Veg•All, beans and chicken broth; heat until hot. Serve immediately.   *Makes 4 to 6 servings*

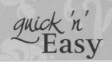
Ravioli Soup

1 package (9 ounces) fresh or frozen cheese ravioli or tortellini
¾ pound hot Italian sausage, crumbled
1 can (14½ ounces) DEL MONTE® Italian Recipe Stewed Tomatoes
1 can (14½ ounces) beef broth
1 can (14½ ounces) DEL MONTE® Cut Italian Green Beans, drained
2 green onions, sliced

1. Cook pasta according to package directions; drain.

2. Meanwhile, cook sausage in 5-quart pot over medium-high heat until no longer pink; drain. Add undrained tomatoes, broth and 1¾ cups water; bring to a boil.

3. Reduce heat to low; stir in pasta, beans and green onions. Simmer until heated through. Season with pepper and sprinkle with grated Parmesan cheese, if desired.   *Makes 4 servings*

Prep and Cook Time: 15 minutes

Hearty Minestrone Soup

2 cans (10¾ ounces each) condensed Italian tomato soup
3 cups water
3 cups cooked vegetables, such as zucchini, peas, corn and beans
2 cups cooked ditalini pasta
1⅓ cups FRENCH'S® French Fried Onions

Combine soup and water in large saucepan. Add vegetables and pasta. Bring to a boil. Reduce heat. Cook until heated through, stirring often.

Place French Fried Onions in microwavable dish. Microwave on HIGH 1 minute or until onions are golden.

Ladle soup into individual bowls. Sprinkle with French Fried Onions.

Makes 6 servings

Prep Time: 10 minutes • **Cook Time:** 5 minutes

Quick Beef Stew in Foil

8 ounces boneless beef top sirloin steak, cut into 1-inch cubes
1 red potato, peeled and cut into ¾-inch cubes
1 cup frozen mixed vegetables
⅔ cup beef gravy
1 teaspoon fresh minced parsley
¼ teaspoon salt
¼ teaspoon dried thyme
⅛ teaspoon black pepper
1 sheet (20×12 inches) heavy-duty foil, lightly sprayed with
    nonstick cooking spray

1. Preheat oven to 450°F.

2. Combine beef, potato, frozen vegetables, gravy, parsley, salt, thyme and pepper in medium bowl; stir to mix.

3. Place beef mixture in center of foil sheet. Double fold sides and ends of foil to seal packet, leaving head space for heat circulation. Place packet on baking sheet.

4. Bake 30 minutes or until beef is tender. Carefully open one end of packet to allow steam to escape. Open packet and transfer stew to two bowls.

Makes 2 servings

tip: Oven temperatures can vary significantly depending on the oven model and manufacturer, so watch your stew carefully and check for doneness using the test given in the recipe.

Quick Broccoli Soup

   4 cups chicken or vegetable broth
2½ pounds broccoli florets
   1 onion, quartered
   1 cup milk
   ¼ teaspoon salt
   ¼ cup crumbled blue cheese

1. Place broth, broccoli and onion in large saucepan; bring to a boil over high heat. Reduce heat to low. Cover and simmer 20 minutes or until vegetables are tender.

2. Place soup in food processor or blender; process until smooth. Return to saucepan. Stir in milk and salt. Sprinkle with cheese.   *Makes 6 servings*

Cream of Asparagus Soup

   1 tablespoon margarine or butter
   1 small onion, chopped
   2 cans (14½ ounces each) chicken broth
   1 jar (1 pound) **RAGÚ® Cheesy!® Classic Alfredo Sauce**
   2 packages (10 ounces each) frozen asparagus spears, thawed

1. In 3½-quart saucepan, melt margarine over medium heat and cook onion, stirring occasionally, 5 minutes or until tender. Stir in broth, Ragú® Cheesy!® Sauce and asparagus. Bring to a boil over medium heat, stirring frequently. Reduce heat to low and simmer 5 minutes or until asparagus is tender.

2. In blender or food processor, purée hot soup mixture until smooth. Return soup to saucepan and heat through. Season, if desired, with salt and ground black pepper.   *Makes 8 servings*

Variation: For Cream of Broccoli Soup, substitute frozen broccoli spears for asparagus.

Serving Suggestion: Serve soup with cheese toast croutons. Simply place Swiss cheese on sliced French bread rounds and broil until cheese is melted.

Prep Time: 5 minutes • **Cook Time:** 20 minutes

Chicken and Wild Rice Soup

   5 cups chicken broth, divided
 ½ cup uncooked wild rice, rinsed and drained
 ¼ cup (½ stick) butter
   1 carrot, sliced
   1 onion, chopped
   2 stalks celery, chopped
 ½ (8-ounce) package mushrooms, sliced
   2 tablespoons all-purpose flour
 ¼ teaspoon salt
 ¼ teaspoon white pepper
 1½ cups chopped cooked chicken
 ¼ cup dry sherry (optional)

1. Combine 2½ cups broth and rice in medium saucepan; bring to a boil. Reduce heat to medium-low. Cover and simmer 1 hour or until rice is tender. Drain; set aside.

2. Melt butter in large saucepan over medium heat. Add carrot; cook and stir 3 minutes. Add onion, celery and mushrooms; cook and stir 3 to 4 minutes or until tender. Whisk in flour, salt and pepper until smooth.

3. Gradually stir in remaining 2½ cups broth; bring to a boil. Reduce heat to medium-low. Cook and stir 2 minutes or until thickened. Stir in chicken, rice and sherry, if desired. Simmer 3 minutes or until heated through. *Makes 4 to 6 servings*

Country Noodle Soup

1 tablespoon **I CAN'T BELIEVE IT'S NOT BUTTER!®** Spread
¾ **cup finely chopped onion**
½ **cup finely chopped red bell pepper**
2½ **cups water**
4 **cups chicken broth or bouillon**
1 **package KNORR® PASTA SIDES™-Chicken Broccoli or Chicken**
½ **cup cut-up cooked chicken, turkey or ham (optional)**

Melt Spread in 4-quart saucepan over medium-high heat and cook onion and red pepper, stirring occasionally, 5 minutes or until tender. Stir in water and chicken broth. Bring just to a boil over high heat. Stir in KNORR® PASTA SIDES™-Chicken Broccoli. Continue boiling over medium heat, stirring occasionally, 8 minutes or until pasta is tender. Stir in chicken; heat through.

Makes 6 servings

Prep Time: 10 minutes • **Cook Time:** 16 minutes

Slow-Cooked Chicken and Mushroom Stew

4 **TYSON® Individually Frozen Boneless Skinless Chicken Breasts**
1 **can (10¾ ounces) cream of mushroom and roasted garlic soup**
  Salt and black pepper, to taste
8 **ounces medium white mushrooms**
1 **cup baby-cut carrots**
2 **celery ribs, cut into 1½-inch lengths**

Slow Cooker Directions

1. Stir together soup and ½ can of water in slow cooker. Wash hands. Cut chicken into 2-inch chunks. Sprinkle with salt and pepper to taste. Put chicken in slow cooker. Wash hands. Add mushrooms, carrots and celery. Stir gently to mix.

2. Cover and cook on LOW 6 to 8 hours or until internal juices of chicken run clear. (Or insert instant-read meat thermometer into thickest part of chicken. Temperature should read 180°F.) Refrigerate leftovers immediately.

Makes 4 servings

Serving Suggestion: Serve with rice sprinkled with parsley.

Prep Time: 10 minutes • **Cook Time:** 6 to 8 hours

Chicken-Barley Soup

    6 cups cold water
1½ pounds chicken thighs, skinned★
    2 stalks celery, sliced
    2 carrots, peeled and thinly sliced
    1 leek, sliced
1½ teaspoons salt
    ½ teaspoon dried marjoram
    ¼ teaspoon black pepper
    ¼ teaspoon dried summer savory
    1 herb bouquet★★
    ⅓ cup quick-cooking barley
    3 cups loosely packed spinach, chopped
    ¼ small red bell pepper, cut into matchsticks
    Celery leaves (optional)

★To skin chicken easily, grasp skin with paper towel and pull away. Repeat with fresh paper towel for each piece of chicken, discarding skins and towels.

★★Use any combination of herbs and spices, such as parsley, thyme sprigs, peppercorns, whole cloves, bay leaves and garlic cloves for herb bouquet. Wrap small bundle in cheesecloth and tie with string.

1. Place water, chicken, celery, carrots, leek, salt, marjoram, black pepper, savory and herb bouquet in 5-quart Dutch oven; bring to a boil. Reduce heat to medium-low. Simmer 45 minutes or until chicken is tender.

2. Remove chicken from soup and cool slightly. Remove herb bouquet; discard. Skim foam and fat from soup using large spoon. Add barley to soup; bring to a boil. Reduce heat to medium-low. Simmer 10 minutes or until barley is almost tender.

3. Meanwhile, remove chicken meat from bones when cool enough to handle; discard bones. Cut chicken into bite-size pieces. Stir chicken, spinach and bell pepper into soup. Simmer 5 minutes or until spinach is wilted and soup is heated through. Garnish with celery leaves. *Makes 6 servings*

My Mother's Sausage & Vegetable Soup

- 1 can (about 15 ounces) black beans, rinsed and drained
- 1 can (about 14 ounces) diced tomatoes
- 1 can (10¾ ounces) condensed cream of mushroom soup, undiluted
- ½ pound turkey sausage, cut into ½-inch slices
- 2 cups diced potato
- 1 cup chopped onion
- 1 cup chopped red bell pepper
- ½ cup water
- 2 teaspoons horseradish
- 2 teaspoons honey
- 1 teaspoon dried basil

Slow Cooker Directions

1. Combine beans, tomatoes, soup, sausage, potato, onion, pepper, water, horseradish, honey and basil in slow cooker, mix well.

2. Cover; cook on LOW 7 to 8 hours. *Makes 6 to 8 servings*

Country Stew

- 2 bags SUCCESS® Brown Rice
- 1 pound ground turkey
- 1 small onion, chopped
- 2 cans (14½ ounces each) tomatoes, cut-up, undrained
- 1 teaspoon pepper
- ½ teaspoon dried basil leaves, crushed
- ½ teaspoon garlic powder
- 1 can (16 ounces) whole kernel corn, drained

Prepare rice according to package directions.

Brown ground turkey with onion in large skillet, stirring occasionally to separate turkey. Add tomatoes, pepper, basil and garlic powder; simmer 20 minutes, stirring occasionally. Stir in rice and corn; heat thoroughly, stirring occasionally. *Makes 8 servings*

Baked Bean Stew

1 cup chopped onion
1 cup chopped green pepper
1 tablespoon vegetable oil
12 ounces boneless skinless chicken breast or tenders, cut into
    ½-inch pieces
2 cans (15 ounces each) baked beans or pork and beans
1 can (15 ounces) garbanzo beans or black-eyes *or* 1½ cups cooked
    dry-packaged garbanzo beans or black-eyes, rinsed, drained
1 can (14½ ounces) diced tomatoes with roasted garlic, undrained
¾ teaspoon dried sage leaves
½ teaspoon ground cumin
    Salt and pepper, to taste

1. Cook onion and green pepper in oil in large saucepan until tender, 3 to 4 minutes. Add chicken and cook over medium heat until browned, 3 to 4 minutes.

2. Add beans, tomatoes and herbs to saucepan; heat to boiling. Reduce heat and simmer, uncovered, 8 to 10 minutes. Season to taste with salt and pepper.

Makes 8 servings

Tip: Frozen chopped onion and green pepper can be used. Stew can be prepared 1 to 2 days in advance; refrigerate, covered. Stew can also be frozen up to 2 months.

Favorite recipe from American Dry Bean Board

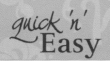
Italian Sausage and Vegetable Stew

1 pound hot or mild Italian sausage links, cut into 1-inch pieces
1 package (16 ounces) frozen vegetable blend, such as onions and
   bell peppers
2 zucchini, sliced
1 can (about 14 ounces) diced Italian-style tomatoes
1 jar (4½ ounces) sliced mushrooms, drained
4 cloves garlic, minced

1. Brown sausage 6 to 8 minutes in large saucepan over medium-high heat, stirring to break up meat. Drain fat.

2. Add frozen vegetables, zucchini, tomatoes, mushrooms and garlic; bring to a boil. Reduce heat to medium-low. Cover and simmer 10 minutes. Cook, uncovered, 5 to 10 minutes or until thickened slightly.   *Makes 6 servings*

Serving Suggestion: Serve with garlic bread.

Prep and Cook Time: 30 minutes

Creamy Asparagus Potato Soup

1 can (14½ ounces) **DEL MONTE®** Whole New Potatoes, drained
1 can (12 ounces) **DEL MONTE** Tender Young Asparagus Spears,
   drained
½ teaspoon dried thyme, crushed
⅛ teaspoon garlic powder
1 can (14 ounces) chicken broth
1 cup milk or half-and-half

1. Place potatoes, asparagus, thyme and garlic powder in food processor or blender (in batches, if needed); process until smooth.

2. Pour into medium saucepan; add broth. Bring to a boil. Stir in milk; heat through. Do not boil. Season with salt and pepper to taste, if desired. Serve hot or cold. Thin with additional milk or water, if desired.   *Makes 4 servings*

Prep Time: 5 minutes • **Cook Time:** 5 minutes

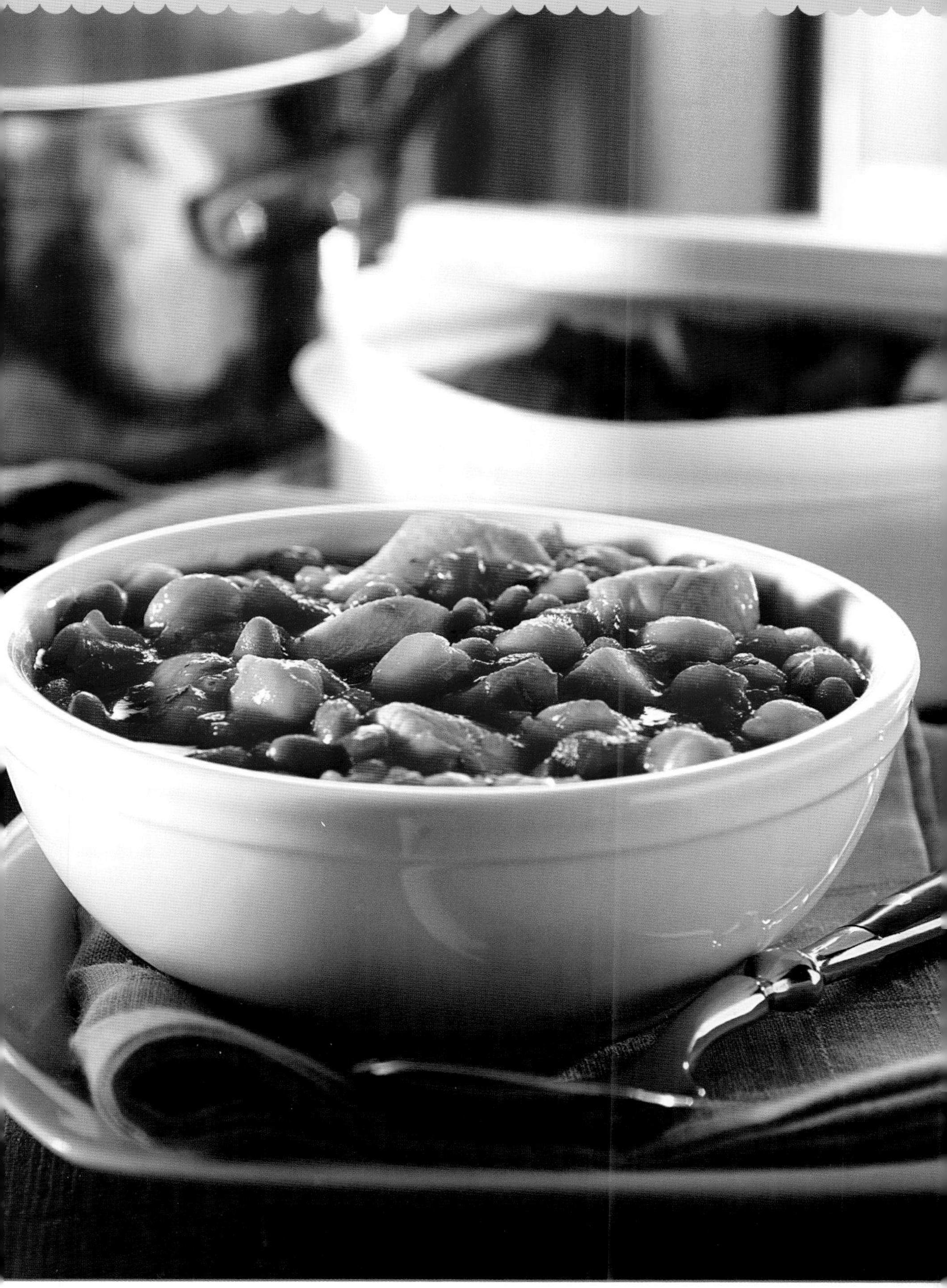

Rich and Hearty Drumstick Soup

2 turkey drumsticks (about 1¾ pounds)
3 carrots, sliced
3 stalks celery, thinly sliced
1 onion, chopped
2 cloves garlic, minced
1 teaspoon poultry seasoning
4 cups chicken broth
3 cups water
8 ounces uncooked egg noodles
⅓ cup chopped fresh Italian parsley
   Salt and black pepper

Slow Cooker Directions

1. Combine drumsticks, carrots, celery, onion, garlic and seasoning in slow cooker. Pour broth and water over top. Cover; cook on HIGH 5 hours or until meat is falling off bones.

2. Remove turkey; set aside. Add noodles to slow cooker. Cover; cook 30 minutes or until tender. Meanwhile, remove turkey meat from bones when cool enough to handle; discard skin and bones. Shred meat using two forks.

3. Return turkey to slow cooker. Cover; cook 5 minutes or until heated through. Stir in parsley. Season with salt and pepper.   *Makes 8 servings*

tip: Slow cooker recipes with raw meats should cook a minimum of 3 hours on LOW OR 1½ hours on HIGH for food safety reasons.

Turkey Mushroom Stew

1 pound turkey cutlets, cut into 4×1-inch strips
1 onion, thinly sliced
2 tablespoons minced green onion
8 ounces mushrooms, sliced
1 cup half-and-half or milk
2 to 3 tablespoons all-purpose flour
1 teaspoon salt
1 teaspoon dried tarragon
   Black pepper
½ cup frozen peas
½ cup sour cream
   Puff pastry shells

Slow Cooker Directions

1. Layer turkey, onion, green onion and mushrooms in slow cooker. Cover; cook on LOW 4 hours.

2. Remove turkey and vegetables to serving bowl. Stir half-and-half, flour, salt, tarragon and pepper in medium bowl until smooth; add to slow cooker. Return turkey and cooked vegetables to slow cooker. Stir in peas.

3. Cover; cook on HIGH 30 to 45 minutes or until sauce is thickened. Stir in sour cream just before serving. Serve in puff pastry shells.

Makes 4 servings

Chicken Stew with Dumplings

2 tablespoons vegetable oil
2 cups sliced carrots
1 cup chopped onion
1 green bell pepper, sliced
½ cup sliced celery
2 cans (about 14 ounces each) chicken broth, divided
¼ cup plus 2 tablespoons all-purpose flour
2 pounds boneless skinless chicken breasts, cut into 1-inch pieces
3 potatoes, unpeeled and cut into 1-inch pieces
6 ounces mushrooms, halved
¾ cup frozen peas
1½ teaspoons dried basil, divided
1¼ teaspoons dried rosemary, divided
½ teaspoon dried tarragon, divided
¾ to 1 teaspoon salt
¼ teaspoon black pepper
2 cups biscuit baking mix
⅔ cup milk

1. Heat oil in large Dutch oven over medium heat. Add carrots, onion, bell pepper and celery; cook and stir 5 minutes or until onion is tender. Reserve ½ cup broth. Stir remaining broth into vegetable mixture; bring to a boil. Mix reserved ½ cup broth and flour in small bowl; stir into Dutch oven. Boil 1 minute or until thickened, stirring constantly. Stir in chicken, potatoes, mushrooms, peas, 1 teaspoon basil, ¾ teaspoon rosemary and ¼ teaspoon tarragon. Reduce heat to medium-low. Simmer, covered, 18 to 20 minutes or until vegetables are almost tender and chicken is cooked through. Add salt and black pepper.

2. Combine biscuit mix, remaining ½ teaspoon basil, ½ teaspoon rosemary and ¼ teaspoon tarragon in small bowl; stir in milk to form soft dough. Evenly spoon dumpling mixture on top of stew in 8 large spoonfuls. Reduce heat to low. Cook, uncovered, 10 minutes. Cover and cook 10 minutes or until dumplings are tender and toothpick inserted into centers comes out clean.

Makes 8 servings

Make-Ahead Time: up to 2 days before serving • **Final Prep and Cook Time:** 30 minutes

Hearty One-Pot Chicken Stew

12 **TYSON®** **Individually Frozen Boneless Skinless Chicken Tenderloins**
 1 **box traditional red beans and rice mix**
2¼ **cups water**
 1 **can (14½ ounces) diced tomatoes, undrained**
 3 **new red potatoes, unpeeled, cut into 1-inch pieces**
 2 **carrots, sliced ½ inch thick**
 1 **onion, cut into 1-inch pieces**

1. Wash hands. Remove protective ice glaze from frozen chicken by holding under cool running water 1 to 2 minutes. Cut into 1-inch pieces. Wash hands.

2. In large saucepan, combine chicken, beans and rice, contents of seasoning packet, water, tomatoes, potatoes, carrots and onion. Bring to a boil. Cover, reduce heat; simmer 20 minutes or until internal juices of chicken run clear. (Or insert instant-read meat thermometer into thickest part of chicken. Temperature should read 180°F.) Refrigerate leftovers.   *Makes 4 servings*

Prep Time: 10 minutes • **Cook Time:** 20 to 25 minutes

Chunky Chicken Vegetable Soup

 1 **teaspoon vegetable oil**
 ½ **pound boneless skinless chicken breasts, cut into ½-inch cubes**
 1 **can (14½ ounces) chicken broth**
 2 **cups water**
 2 **cups assorted cut-up vegetables (sliced carrots, broccoli florets,**
      chopped red bell pepper)★
 1 **packet Italian salad dressing and recipe mix**
 1 **cup MINUTE® White Rice, uncooked**
 2 **tablespoons fresh parsley, chopped**

★*Or substitute 1 package (10 ounces) frozen mixed vegetables, thawed.*

Heat oil in large saucepan over medium-high heat. Add chicken; cook and stir until browned.

Add broth, water, vegetables and salad dressing mix. Bring to a boil. Reduce heat to low; cover. Simmer 5 minutes.

Stir in rice and parsley; cover. Remove from heat. Let stand 5 minutes.

Makes 4 servings

Turkey Vegetable Rice Soup

1½ **pounds turkey drumsticks**
8 **cups cold water**
1 **onion, cut into quarters**
2 **tablespoons soy sauce**
¼ **teaspoon black pepper**
1 **bay leaf**
2 **carrots, sliced**
⅓ **cup uncooked rice**
4 **ounces mushrooms, sliced**
1 **cup snow peas, cut in half crosswise**
1 **cup coarsely chopped bok choy**

1. Place turkey in 5-quart Dutch oven. Add water, onion, soy sauce, pepper and bay leaf; bring to a boil over high heat. Reduce heat to medium-low. Simmer 1½ hours or until turkey is tender.

2. Remove turkey from Dutch oven; cool broth. Skim fat; discard bay leaf. Remove turkey meat from bones when cool enough to handle; discard skin and bones. Cut turkey into bite-size pieces.

3. Add carrots and rice to Dutch oven; bring to a boil over high heat. Reduce heat to medium-low. Simmer 10 minutes.

4. Add mushrooms and turkey to soup; bring to a boil over high heat. Reduce heat to medium-low. Simmer 5 minutes.

5. Stir snow peas and bok choy into soup; bring to a boil over high heat. Reduce heat to medium-low. Simmer 8 minutes or until rice and vegetables are tender. *Makes 6 servings*

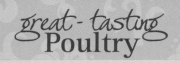
Apple and Chicken Soup

- 1 sweet potato
- 1 tablespoon olive oil
- 2 stalks celery, thinly sliced
- $\frac{1}{2}$ medium onion, chopped
- 1 teaspoon dried thyme
- $\frac{1}{2}$ teaspoon dried rosemary
- $\frac{1}{4}$ teaspoon dried sage
- $\frac{1}{4}$ teaspoon ground nutmeg
- 2 cans (about 14 ounces each) chicken broth
- 1 cup apple juice
- 1 McIntosh apple, peeled and chopped
- $\frac{2}{3}$ cup uncooked small pasta shells
- $\frac{3}{4}$ pound boneless skinless chicken breasts, cut into $\frac{1}{4}$-inch strips

1. Pierce sweet potato all over with fork. Microwave on HIGH 6 minutes or until crisp-tender; let stand. (Sweet potato will finish cooking and become tender as it stands.)

2. Heat oil in large saucepan over medium-high heat. Add celery, onion, thyme, rosemary, sage and nutmeg. Cover; cook 3 minutes or until onion is tender. Add broth, juice and apple; bring to a boil. Stir in pasta; cook, uncovered, 8 to 10 minutes.

3. Peel skin from sweet potato; cut into 1-inch pieces. Add chicken and sweet potato to soup. Reduce heat to medium-low. Simmer 5 minutes or until chicken is cooked through and pasta is tender.   *Makes 4 to 6 servings*

Prep and Cook Time: 25 minutes

Country Turkey and Veggie Soup with Cream

2 tablespoons butter, divided
8 ounces sliced mushrooms
½ cup chopped onion
½ cup thinly sliced celery
1 red bell pepper, chopped
1 carrot, thinly sliced
½ teaspoon dried thyme
4 cups chicken or turkey broth
2 cups chopped cooked turkey
4 ounces uncooked egg noodles
1 cup half-and-half
½ cup frozen peas, thawed
¾ teaspoon salt

Slow Cooker Directions

1. Melt 1 tablespoon butter in large nonstick skillet over medium-high heat. Add mushrooms and onion; cook and stir 4 minutes or until onion is translucent. Transfer mixture to slow cooker. Add celery, bell pepper, carrot and thyme to slow cooker; pour in broth.

2. Cover; cook on HIGH 2½ hours.

3. Add turkey and noodles; cook, covered, 20 minutes. Stir in half-and-half, peas, remaining 1 tablespoon butter and salt. Cook 5 minutes or until noodles are tender. *Makes 8 servings*

Chicken Rotini Soup

½ **pound boneless skinless chicken breasts, cut into** ½**-inch pieces**
4 **cups chicken broth**
2 **tablespoons butter**
½ **onion, chopped**
4 **ounces mushrooms, sliced**
1 **teaspoon Worcestershire sauce**
¼ **teaspoon dried tarragon**
¾ **cup uncooked rotini pasta**
1 **zucchini, cut into** ⅛**-inch slices**

1. Combine chicken and broth in medium saucepan; bring to a boil over high heat. Reduce heat to medium-low. Simmer 2 minutes; set aside.

2. Melt butter in 5-quart Dutch oven or large saucepan over medium heat. Add onion and mushrooms; cook and stir until onion is tender. Stir in chicken mixture, Worcestershire sauce and tarragon; bring to a boil over high heat. Stir in pasta. Reduce heat to medium-low. Simmer 5 minutes.

3. Add zucchini to soup; simmer 5 minutes or until pasta is tender.

Makes 4 servings

tip: If you skin and debone your own chicken breasts, be sure to reserve both the bones and the skin. Let these scraps collect in a plastic bag in your freezer and soon you'll have enough to make flavorful homemade chicken stock.

Creamy Farmhouse Chicken and Garden Soup

½ **package (16 ounces) frozen stir-fry vegetables**
1 **cup frozen corn, thawed**
1 **zucchini, sliced**
2 **bone-in chicken thighs, skinned★**
1 **can (about 14 ounces) chicken broth**
½ **teaspoon minced garlic**
½ **teaspoon dried thyme**
2 **ounces uncooked egg noodles**
1 **cup half-and-half**
½ **cup frozen peas**
2 **tablespoons finely chopped fresh parsley**
2 **tablespoons butter**
1 **teaspoon salt**
½ **teaspoon black pepper**

★To skin chicken easily, grasp skin with paper towel and pull away. Repeat with fresh paper towel for each piece of chicken, discarding skins and towels.

Slow Cooker Directions

1. Combine stir-fry vegetables, corn and zucchini in slow cooker. Add chicken, broth, garlic and thyme. Cover; cook on HIGH 3 to 4 hours or until chicken is no longer pink in center. Remove chicken; cool slightly.

2. Add noodles to slow cooker. Cover; cook 20 minutes or until almost tender.

3. Meanwhile, remove chicken meat from bones when cool enough to handle; discard bones. Cut chicken into bite-size pieces. Return chicken to slow cooker. Stir in half-and-half, peas, parsley, butter, salt and pepper. Let stand 5 minutes before serving. *Makes 4 servings*

Prep Time: 15 minutes • **Cook Time:** 3 to 4 hours, plus 25 minutes

Vegetarian

Italian Hillside Garden Soup

1 tablespoon olive oil
1 cup chopped onion
1 cup chopped green bell pepper
½ cup sliced celery
2 cans (about 14 ounces each) vegetable broth
1 can (about 15 ounces) navy beans, rinsed and drained
1 can (about 14 ounces) diced tomatoes with basil, garlic and
    oregano
1 zucchini, chopped
1 cup frozen cut green beans, thawed
¼ teaspoon garlic powder
1 package (9 ounces) refrigerated cheese tortellini
3 tablespoons chopped fresh basil
    Grated Asiago or Parmesan cheese (optional)

Slow Cooker Directions

1. Heat oil in large skillet over medium-high heat. Add onion, pepper and celery; cook and stir 4 minutes or until onion is translucent. Transfer to 5-quart slow cooker.

2. Add broth, navy beans, tomatoes, zucchini, green beans and garlic powder. Cover; cook on LOW 7 hours or on HIGH 3½ hours.

3. *Turn slow cooker to HIGH.* Add tortellini; cook 20 minutes or until tender. Stir in basil. Sprinkle with cheese just before serving.

Makes 6 servings

Prep Time: 15 minutes • **Cook Time:** 7 hours (LOW) or
3½ hours (HIGH)

Fresh Lime and Black Bean Soup

2 cans (about 15 ounces each) black beans, undrained
1 can (about 14 ounces) vegetable broth
1½ cups chopped onions
1½ teaspoons chili powder
¾ teaspoon ground cumin
¼ teaspoon garlic powder
⅛ to ¼ teaspoon red pepper flakes
½ cup sour cream
2 tablespoons extra virgin olive oil
2 tablespoons chopped fresh cilantro
1 lime, cut into wedges

Slow Cooker Directions

1. Coat slow cooker with nonstick cooking spray. Add beans, broth, onions, chili powder, cumin, garlic powder and red pepper flakes.

2. Cover; cook on LOW 7 hours or on HIGH 3½ hours.

3. To thicken soup, place half of soup mixture in food processor or blender; process until smooth. Stir into remaining soup in slow cooker. Let stand 15 to 20 minutes before serving.

4. Serve soup with sour cream, oil, cilantro and lime wedges.

Makes 4 servings

Prep Time: 10 minutes • **Cook Time:** 7 hours (LOW) or 3½ hours (HIGH)

Potato Cheddar Soup

2 pounds new red potatoes, cut into ½-inch cubes
3 cups vegetable broth
¾ cup coarsely chopped carrots
1 onion, coarsely chopped
½ teaspoon salt
1 cup half-and-half
¼ teaspoon black pepper
2 cups (8 ounces) shredded Cheddar cheese

Slow Cooker Directions

1. Place potatoes, broth, carrots, onion and salt in slow cooker.

2. Cover; cook on LOW 6 to 7 hours or on HIGH 3 to 3½ hours.

3. *Turn slow cooker to HIGH.* Stir in half-and-half and pepper. Cover; cook 15 minutes. Turn off heat. Let stand, uncovered, 5 minutes. Stir in cheese.

Makes 6 servings

Italian Skillet Roasted Vegetable Soup

2 tablespoons olive oil, divided
1 red, yellow or orange bell pepper, chopped
1 clove garlic, minced
2 cups water
1 can (about 14 ounces) diced tomatoes
1 zucchini, thinly sliced
⅛ teaspoon red pepper flakes
1 can (about 15 ounces) navy beans, rinsed and drained
3 to 4 tablespoons chopped fresh basil
1 tablespoon balsamic vinegar
¾ teaspoon salt

1. Heat 1 tablespoon oil in Dutch oven over medium-high heat. Add bell pepper; cook and stir 4 minutes or until edges are browned. Add garlic; cook and stir 15 seconds. Add water, tomatoes, zucchini and red pepper flakes; bring to a boil over high heat. Reduce heat to medium-low. Cover and simmer 20 minutes.

2. Add beans, basil, remaining 1 tablespoon oil, vinegar and salt; remove from heat. Let stand, covered, 10 minutes before serving. *Makes 5 servings*

Chickpea and Orange Squash Stew

1 teaspoon canola oil
¾ cup chopped onion
½ to 1 jalapeño pepper,★ seeded and minced
1 (½-inch) piece fresh ginger, peeled and minced
1 clove garlic, minced
2 teaspoons ground cumin
½ teaspoon ground coriander
1 cup cubed peeled orange squash, sweet potato or pumpkin
1 cup canned chickpeas, rinsed and drained
½ cup water
1½ teaspoons soy sauce
1 cup coconut milk
¼ cup chopped fresh cilantro
Juice of 1 lime
Spinach leaves (optional)

★*Jalapeño peppers can sting and irritate the skin, so wear rubber gloves when handling peppers and do not touch your eyes.*

1. Heat oil in medium saucepan over medium-low heat. Add onion, jalapeño, ginger and garlic; cook and stir 2 to 3 minutes or until onion is translucent. Add cumin and coriander; cook and stir 1 minute.

2. Add squash, chickpeas, water and soy sauce to saucepan; bring to a boil. Reduce heat to medium-low. Simmer 15 minutes or until squash is tender. Add coconut milk; cook and stir 2 to 3 minutes or until heated through. Stir in cilantro and lime juice. Garnish with spinach.   *Makes 2 servings*

Mushroom Barley Stew

1 tablespoon olive oil
1 onion, finely chopped
1 cup chopped carrots
1 clove garlic, minced
5 cups vegetable broth
1 cup uncooked pearl barley
1 cup dried wild mushrooms, broken into pieces
1 teaspoon salt
$\frac{1}{2}$ teaspoon dried thyme
$\frac{1}{2}$ teaspoon black pepper

Slow Cooker Directions

1. Heat oil in medium skillet over medium-high heat. Add onion, carrots and garlic; cook and stir 5 minutes or until tender. Transfer to slow cooker. Add broth, barley, mushrooms, salt, thyme and pepper to slow cooker; stir well to combine.

2. Cover; cook on LOW 6 to 7 hours. *Makes 4 to 6 servings*

Variation: To turn this thick, robust stew into a soup, add 2 to 3 additional cups of broth. Cook for the same length of time.

Prep Time: 10 minutes • **Cook Time:** 6 to 7 hours

Rustic Vegetable Soup

1 to 2 baking potatoes, cut into ½-inch pieces
1 jar (16 ounces) picante sauce
1 package (10 ounces) frozen mixed vegetables, thawed
1 package (10 ounces) frozen cut green beans, thawed
1 green bell pepper, chopped
1 can (about 10 ounces) condensed vegetable broth, undiluted
½ teaspoon sugar
¼ cup finely chopped fresh parsley

Slow Cooker Directions

1. Combine potatoes, picante sauce, mixed vegetables, beans, pepper, broth and sugar in slow cooker.

2. Cover; cook on LOW 8 hours or on HIGH 4 hours. Stir in parsley.

Makes 8 servings

Vegetable and Red Lentil Soup

1 can (about 14 ounces) vegetable broth
1 can (about 14 ounces) diced tomatoes
2 zucchini or yellow summer squash (or 1 of each), chopped
1 red or yellow bell pepper, chopped
½ cup thinly sliced carrots
½ cup dried red lentils, rinsed and sorted*
½ teaspoon salt
½ teaspoon sugar
¼ teaspoon black pepper
2 tablespoons chopped fresh basil or thyme
½ cup croutons (optional)

If you have difficulty finding red lentils, substitute brown lentils.

Slow Cooker Directions

1. Combine broth, tomatoes, zucchini, bell pepper, carrots, lentils, salt, sugar and black pepper in slow cooker.

2. Cover; cook on LOW 8 hours or on HIGH 4 hours. Top with basil and croutons, if desired.

Makes 4 servings

Lentil Stew over Couscous

3 cups dried lentils (1 pound), rinsed and sorted

3 cups water

1 can (about 14 ounces) vegetable broth

1 can (about 14 ounces) diced tomatoes

1 onion, chopped

1 green bell pepper, chopped

4 stalks celery, chopped

1 carrot, halved lengthwise and sliced

2 cloves garlic, chopped

1 teaspoon dried marjoram

¼ teaspoon black pepper

1 tablespoon olive oil

1 tablespoon apple cider vinegar

4½ to 5 cups hot cooked couscous

Slow Cooker Directions

1. Combine lentils, water, broth, tomatoes, onion, bell pepper, celery, carrot, garlic, marjoram and black pepper in slow cooker.

2. Cover; cook on LOW 8 to 9 hours. Stir in oil and vinegar. Serve over couscous. *Makes 12 servings*

Tip: Lentil stew keeps well in the refrigerator for up to 1 week. Stew can also be frozen in an airtight container for up to 3 months.

Prep Time: 10 minutes • **Cook Time:** 8 to 9 hours

Curried Sweet Potato and Carrot Soup

2 sweet potatoes, peeled and cut into ¾-inch cubes (about 5 cups)
2 cups baby carrots
1 onion, chopped
¾ teaspoon curry powder
½ teaspoon salt
½ teaspoon ground cinnamon
½ teaspoon black pepper
¼ teaspoon ground ginger
4 cups vegetable broth
¾ cup half-and-half
1 tablespoon maple syrup
    Candied ginger (optional)

Slow Cooker Directions

1. Place sweet potatoes, carrots, onion, curry powder, salt, cinnamon, pepper and ground ginger in slow cooker. Add broth.

2. Cover; cook on LOW 7 to 8 hours.

3. Working in batches, process soup in food processor or blender until smooth. Return to slow cooker. (Or use immersion blender.) Add half-and-half and maple syrup. Cover; cook on HIGH 15 minutes or until heated through. Garnish with candied ginger. *Makes 8 servings*

Prep Time: 10 minutes • **Cook Time:** 7 to 8 hours

tip: An immersion blender serves some of the same functions as a regular blender, but has the added convenience of being submerged in slow cookers, saucepans, bowls and glasses.

Chickpea-Vegetable Soup

1 teaspoon olive oil
1 cup chopped onion
$\frac{1}{2}$ cup chopped green bell pepper
2 cloves garlic, minced
2 cans (about 14 ounces each) diced tomatoes
3 cups water
2 cups broccoli florets
1 can (about 15 ounces) chickpeas, rinsed, drained and slightly mashed
$\frac{1}{2}$ cup (3 ounces) orzo or rosamarina pasta
1 bay leaf
1 tablespoon chopped fresh thyme *or* 1 teaspoon dried thyme
1 tablespoon chopped fresh rosemary *or* 1 teaspoon dried rosemary
1 tablespoon lime juice or lemon juice
$\frac{1}{2}$ teaspoon ground turmeric
$\frac{1}{4}$ teaspoon salt
$\frac{1}{4}$ teaspoon ground red pepper
$\frac{1}{4}$ cup toasted pumpkin seeds or sunflower kernels

1. Heat oil in large saucepan over medium heat. Add onion, bell pepper and garlic; cook and stir until vegetables are tender.

2. Add tomatoes, water, broccoli, chickpeas, orzo, bay leaf, thyme, rosemary, lime juice, turmeric, salt and red pepper; bring to a boil over high heat. Reduce heat to medium-low. Cover and simmer 10 to 12 minutes or until orzo is tender.

3. Remove and discard bay leaf. Sprinkle with pumpkin seeds.

Makes 4 servings

Bean Soup Provençale

¼ **cup vegetable oil**
1½ **cups chopped onion**
1½ **cups chopped celery**
1 **cup sliced leeks**
8 **cups water**
1 **cup sliced carrots**
1 **turnip, peeled and diced**
1 **teaspoon salt**
¼ **teaspoon black pepper**
    Pesto Sauce (recipe follows)
2 **cans (about 15 ounces each) great Northern beans,★ rinsed and
    drained**
1 **zucchini, sliced**
1 **cup sliced fresh or frozen chopped spinach**

★*Substitute 3⅓ cups drained cooked dried beans.*

1. Heat ¼ cup oil in large saucepan over medium heat. Add onion, celery and leeks; cook and stir 10 minutes or until onion is softened. Add water, carrots, turnip, salt and pepper; bring to a boil over high heat. Reduce heat to low. Cover and simmer 30 minutes or until vegetables are tender.

2. Meanwhile, prepare Pesto Sauce.

3. Stir in beans, zucchini and spinach until heated through. Top with Pesto Sauce.   *Makes 8 to 10 servings*

Pesto Sauce

½ **cup chopped parsley**
¼ **cup olive oil**
¼ **grated Parmesan cheese**
1 **to 2 cloves garlic**
1 **tablespoon dried basil**
1 **teaspoon lemon juice**

Place parsley, ¼ cup oil, cheese, garlic, basil and lemon juice in blender or food processor; process until smooth.   *Makes about ⅓ cup*

Slow Cooker Veggie Stew

    1 tablespoon vegetable oil
$^2/_3$ cup carrot slices
$^1/_2$ cup diced onion
    2 cloves garlic, chopped
    2 cans (about 14 ounces each) vegetable broth
$1^1/_2$ cups chopped green cabbage
$^1/_2$ cup cut green beans
$^1/_2$ cup diced zucchini
    1 tablespoon tomato paste
$^1/_2$ teaspoon dried basil
$^1/_2$ teaspoon dried oregano
$^1/_4$ teaspoon salt

Slow Cooker Directions

1. Heat oil in medium skillet over medium-high heat. Add carrot, onion and garlic; cook and stir until tender. Place carrot mixture, broth, cabbage, beans, zucchini, tomato paste, basil, oregano and salt in slow cooker.

2. Cover; cook on LOW 8 to 10 hours or on HIGH 4 to 5 hours.

Makes 4 to 6 servings

Italian Escarole and White Bean Stew

1 tablespoon olive oil
1 onion, chopped
3 carrots, cut into ½-inch-thick rounds
2 cloves garlic, minced
1 can (about 14 ounces) vegetable broth
1 head (about 12 ounces) escarole
¼ teaspoon red pepper flakes
2 cans (about 15 ounces each) Great Northern white beans,
    rinsed and drained
Salt
Grated Parmesan cheese (optional)

Slow Cooker Directions

1. Heat oil in medium skillet over medium-high heat. Add onion and carrots; cook 5 minutes or until onion is softened, stirring occasionally. Add garlic; cook and stir 1 minute. Transfer to slow cooker. Pour in broth.

2. Trim base of escarole. Roughly cut crosswise into 1-inch wide strips. Wash well in large bowl of cold water. Lift out by handfuls, leaving sand or dirt in bottom of bowl. Shake to remove excess water, but do not dry. Add to slow cooker. Sprinkle with red pepper flakes. Top with beans.

3. Cover; cook on LOW 7 to 8 hours or on HIGH 3½ to 4 hours. Season with salt. Sprinkle with cheese, if desired.   *Makes 4 servings*

tip: Escarole is very leafy and easily fills a 4½-quart slow cooker when raw, but it shrinks dramatically as it cooks down. This recipe makes 4 portions, but can easily be doubled. Simply double the quantities of all the ingredients listed and be sure to use a 6-quart (or larger) slow cooker.

Navy Vegetable Soup with Tortilla Crisps

1 cup dried navy beans, rinsed and sorted
3 cups water
1 teaspoon salt, divided
6 cups vegetable broth
2 leeks, cut into ½-inch pieces
¾ pound unpeeled new potatoes
2 cups sliced mushrooms
1½ cups thinly sliced carrots
1½ teaspoons dried thyme
1 bay leaf
½ teaspoon black pepper
2 (6-inch) corn tortillas
2 teaspoons olive oil
¼ teaspoon garlic salt
2 tomatoes, seeded and chopped

1. Place beans in large saucepan. Add water. Bring to a boil over high heat. Cover and remove from heat. Let stand 30 minutes. Return to a boil over high heat. Reduce heat to low. Cover and simmer 30 minutes; stir in ½ teaspoon salt. Cover and simmer 1 hour; drain.

2. Add broth, leeks, potatoes, mushrooms, carrots, thyme, bay leaf, remaining ½ teaspoon salt and pepper to Dutch oven; bring to a boil over high heat. Reduce heat to medium-low. Cover and simmer 25 minutes. Add beans; cook 5 minutes. Remove and discard bay leaf.

3. Preheat oven to 425°F. Brush tortillas on both sides with oil; sprinkle top of each with garlic salt. Cut into ¼-inch-wide strips. Arrange on baking sheet; bake 5 to 6 minutes or until crisp. Cool. Sprinkle soup with tomatoes and tortilla crisps. *Makes 8 servings*

Casseroles

Table of Contents

Chili Spaghetti Casserole

  8 ounces uncooked spaghetti
  1 pound ground beef
  1 onion, chopped
  ¼ teaspoon salt
  ⅛ teaspoon black pepper
  1 can (about 15 ounces) vegetarian chili with beans
  1 can (about 14 ounces) Italian-style stewed tomatoes,
      undrained
1½ cups (6 ounces) shredded sharp Cheddar cheese,
      divided
  ½ cup sour cream
1½ teaspoons chili powder
  ¼ teaspoon garlic powder

1. Preheat oven to 350°F. Spray 13×9-inch baking dish with nonstick cooking spray.

2. Cook pasta according to package directions. Drain and place in prepared dish.

3. Meanwhile, place beef and onion in large skillet; season with salt and pepper. Brown beef mixture 6 to 8 minutes over medium-high heat, stirring to break up meat. Drain fat. Stir in chili, tomatoes with juice, 1 cup cheese, sour cream, chili powder and garlic powder.

4. Add chili mixture to pasta; stir until pasta is well coated. Sprinkle with remaining ½ cup cheese.

5. Cover tightly with foil and bake 30 minutes or until bubbly and heated through. Let stand 5 minutes before serving.

Makes 8 servings

Beef Pot Pie with Beer Biscuits

4 bacon slices, coarsely chopped
2½ pounds beef chuck, cut into 1-inch cubes
    Salt and black pepper
1 onion, chopped
3 carrots, cut into ½-inch rounds
3 celery stalks, cut into ½-inch rounds
2 cloves garlic, minced
2⅓ cups plus 1 tablespoon all-purpose flour, divided
1 can (about 14 ounces) beef broth
2 tablespoons Worcestershire sauce
1 teaspoon dried thyme
2½ teaspoons baking powder
    ¼ cup plus 2 tablespoons butter, cut into ½-inch cubes
    ¾ cup lager

1. Preheat oven to 350°F. Cook bacon in Dutch oven over medium heat until crisp and browned. Drain on paper towels. Drain all but 2 tablespoons fat from Dutch oven.

2. Season beef with salt and pepper. Brown beef in batches 5 minutes in Dutch oven over medium-high heat. Transfer to plate with slotted spoon; reserve fat in Dutch oven.

3. Add onion, carrots, celery and garlic; cook and stir over medium heat 5 minutes or until vegetables are tender. Sprinkle with ⅓ cup plus 1 tablespoon flour; stir well. Stir in bacon, beef, broth, Worcestershire sauce and thyme; bring to a boil. Cover and bake 1½ hours or until beef is almost tender.

4. Whisk 2 cups flour, baking powder and salt in medium bowl. Cut in butter with pastry blender or two knives until mixture resembles coarse crumbs. Stir in enough lager to make soft dough. Turn dough out onto lightly floured work surface. Roll dough into 9×6-inch rectangle about ½ inch thick. Cut into six 3-inch square biscuits.

5. *Increase oven temperature to 400°F.* Place biscuits over stew, overlapping if needed. Bake 20 minutes or until biscuits are golden brown. *Makes 6 servings*

Patchwork Casserole

2 pounds ground beef
2 cups chopped green bell peppers
1 cup chopped onion
2 pounds frozen Southern-style hash brown potatoes,
thawed
2 cans (8 ounces each) tomato sauce
1 cup water
1 can (6 ounces) tomato paste
1 teaspoon salt
½ teaspoon dried basil
¼ teaspoon black pepper
1 pound thinly sliced pasteurized process cheese product,
divided

1. Preheat oven to 350°F.

2. Brown beef 6 to 8 minutes in large skillet over medium-high heat, stirring to break up meat. Drain all but 1 tablespoon fat. Add bell peppers and onion; cook and stir 4 minutes or until tender. Stir in potatoes, tomato sauce, water, tomato paste, salt, basil and black pepper.

3. Spoon half of mixture into 13×9-inch baking dish; top with half of cheese slices. Spoon remaining beef mixture evenly over top. Cover with foil; bake 45 minutes.

4. Cut remaining cheese slices into decorative shapes; place on top of casserole. Cover and let stand 5 minutes or until cheese is melted. *Makes 8 to 10 servings*

Stuffed Bell Peppers

1 cup chopped fresh tomatoes

1 jalapeño pepper,* seeded and chopped (optional)

1 teaspoon chopped fresh cilantro

1 clove garlic, finely minced

½ teaspoon dried oregano, divided

¼ teaspoon ground cumin

6 ounces ground beef

½ cup cooked brown rice

2 egg whites

2 tablespoons finely chopped onion

¼ teaspoon salt

⅛ teaspoon black pepper

2 large bell peppers, cut in half lengthwise and seeded

Jalapeño peppers can sting and irritate the skin, so wear rubber gloves when handling peppers and do not touch your eyes.

1. Preheat oven to 400°F.

2. Combine tomatoes, jalapeño, if desired, cilantro, garlic, ¼ teaspoon oregano and cumin in small bowl. Set aside.

3. Combine beef, rice, egg whites, onion, salt and black pepper in large bowl. Stir in ⅔ cup tomato mixture. Spoon filling evenly into bell pepper halves.

4. Spray 4 (12×12-inch) sheets heavy-duty foil with nonstick cooking spray. Place each pepper half on foil sheet. Double fold sides and ends of foil to seal packets. Place packets on baking sheet.

5. Bake 45 minutes or until meat is browned and vegetables are tender. Remove from oven. Carefully open one end of each packet to allow steam to escape. Open packets and transfer pepper halves to serving plates. Serve with remaining tomato mixture.

Makes 4 servings

Macaroni & Cheese with Bacon & Tomatoes

Prep Time: 15 minutes | Cook Time: 25 minutes

4 thick slices applewood smoked bacon, diced

2 tablespoons all-purpose flour

2¼ cups milk

½ teaspoon salt

⅛ teaspoon cayenne pepper

1¾ cups (7 ounces) SARGENTO® Shredded Colby-Jack Cheese, divided

8 ounces (2 cups dry) multi-grain or regular elbow macaroni, cooked and drained

1 can (14 ounces) fire-roasted diced tomatoes, drained

COOK bacon in a large saucepan over medium heat 5 to 6 minutes or until crisp, stirring frequently. Use a slotted spoon to transfer bacon to a paper towel; set aside.

ADD flour to drippings in pan; cook and stir 30 seconds. Add milk, salt and cayenne pepper; bring to a boil. Simmer 1 minute or until sauce thickens, stirring frequently. Remove from heat; stir in 1¼ cups cheese until melted. Stir in cooked macaroni and tomatoes. Transfer to a sprayed 9-inch baking dish or shallow 1½-quart casserole.

BAKE in a preheated 375°F oven 20 minutes or until heated through. Sprinkle reserved bacon and remaining cheese over macaroni; continue to bake 5 minutes or until cheese is melted.

Makes 6 servings

Heartland Shepherd's Pie

Prep Time: 5 minutes | Cook Time: 30 minutes

¾ pound ground beef
1 medium onion, chopped
1 can (14½ ounces) DEL MONTE® Original Recipe Stewed
Tomatoes
1 can (8 ounces) DEL MONTE® Tomato Sauce
1 can (14½ ounces) DEL MONTE® Mixed Vegetables,
drained
Instant mashed potato flakes plus ingredients to
prepare (enough for 6 servings)
3 cloves garlic, minced (optional)

1. Preheat oven to 375°F. In large skillet, brown meat and onion over medium-high heat; drain.

2. Add tomatoes and tomato sauce; cook over high heat until thickened, stirring frequently. Stir in mixed vegetables. Season with salt and pepper, if desired.

3. Spoon into 2-quart baking dish; set aside. Prepare 6 servings mashed potatoes according to package directions, first cooking garlic in specified amount of butter.

4. Top meat mixture with potatoes. Bake 20 minutes or until heated through. Garnish with chopped parsley, if desired.

Makes 4 to 6 servings

Pork with Savory Apple Stuffing

Prep Time: 10 minutes | Cook Time: 45 minutes

1 package (6 ounces) corn bread stuffing mix
1 can (14½ ounces) chicken broth
1 small apple, peeled, cored and chopped
¼ cup chopped celery
1⅓ cups FRENCH'S® French Fried Onions, divided
4 boneless pork chops, ¾ inch thick (about 1 pound)
½ cup peach-apricot sweet & sour sauce
1 tablespoon FRENCH'S® Honey Dijon Mustard

1. Preheat oven to 375°F. Combine stuffing mix, broth, apple, celery and ⅔ *cup* French Fried Onions in large bowl. Spoon into bottom of greased shallow 2-quart baking dish. Arrange chops on top of stuffing.

2. Combine sweet & sour sauce with mustard in small bowl. Pour over pork. Bake 40 minutes or until pork is no longer pink in center. Sprinkle with remaining onions. Bake 5 minutes or until onions are golden. *Makes 4 servings*

Bacon and Eggs Brunch Casserole

Prep Time: 15 minutes | Cook Time: 35 minutes

1 tube (8 ounces) refrigerated crescent roll dough
6 eggs
½ cup milk
1 cup (4 ounces) SARGENTO® Chef Style Shredded Mild Cheddar Cheese
8 slices bacon, diced and cooked crisp

SPRAY 13×9-inch baking pan with nonstick cooking spray. Unroll dough and press into bottom of pan. Bake in preheated 350°F oven 10 minutes.

BEAT together eggs and milk in medium bowl. Pour over partially baked dough. Sprinkle with cheese and bacon; return to oven and bake 25 minutes more or until center is set. *Makes 6 servings*

Taco Casserole

2 pounds ground beef
1 can (10 ounces) diced tomatoes with green chiles
1 teaspoon salt
1 teaspoon garlic powder
1 teaspoon ground cumin
1 teaspoon paprika
1 teaspoon chili powder
½ teaspoon ground red pepper
½ teaspoon red pepper flakes
1 bag (12 ounces) nacho cheese tortilla chips, crushed
½ cup chopped green onions
1 cup (4 ounces) shredded Mexican cheese blend
½ cup sour cream (optional)

1. Preheat oven to 375°F.

2. Brown beef 6 to 8 minutes in large skillet over medium-high heat, stirring to break up meat. Drain fat. Stir in tomatoes, salt, garlic powder, cumin, paprika, chili powder, ground red pepper and red pepper flakes; cook 3 minutes.

3. Stir in chips. Transfer to 13×9-inch casserole.

4. Bake 15 to 20 minutes or until heated through. Sprinkle with green onions and cheese. Serve with sour cream, if desired.

Makes 4 to 6 servings

City Pork BBQ Casserole

2 tablespoons vegetable oil
6 to 8 boneless pork chops (about 2 pounds),
    cut into bite-size pieces
¼ cup chopped onion
2 cloves garlic, chopped
2 cups water
2 cups uncooked instant white rice
1 bottle (12 ounces) chili sauce
1 cup ketchup
½ cup packed brown sugar
2 tablespoons honey
1 tablespoon Worcestershire sauce
1 tablespoon hot pepper jelly
1 teaspoon ground ginger
1 teaspoon liquid smoke (optional)
½ teaspoon curry powder
¼ teaspoon black pepper
2 cups (8 ounces) shredded mozzarella cheese

1. Preheat oven to 350°F.

2. Heat oil in large skillet over medium-high heat. Add pork; cook and stir 10 to 15 minutes or until browned and barely pink in center. Add onion and garlic; cook and stir until tender. Drain fat.

3. Meanwhile, bring water to a boil in small saucepan. Stir in rice; cover. Remove from heat; let stand 5 minutes or until water is absorbed.

4. Combine chili sauce, ketchup, brown sugar, honey, Worcestershire sauce, hot pepper jelly, ginger, liquid smoke, if desired, curry powder and black pepper in medium saucepan; bring to a boil over medium-high heat. Reduce heat to low; cover and simmer 10 minutes, stirring occasionally.

5. Combine pork mixture, rice and chili sauce mixture in 2½-quart casserole; mix well. Bake 15 to 20 minutes. Top with cheese; bake 5 minutes or until cheese is melted. Let stand 5 minutes before serving. *Makes 6 to 8 servings*

Beef & Zucchini Quiche

1 unbaked 9-inch pie crust
½ pound ground beef
1 zucchini, shredded
1 cup sliced mushrooms
3 green onions, sliced
1 tablespoon all-purpose flour
1 cup milk
¾ cup (3 ounces) shredded Swiss cheese
3 eggs, beaten
1½ teaspoons chopped fresh thyme *or* ½ teaspoon
    dried thyme
½ teaspoon salt
   Dash black pepper
   Dash ground red pepper

1. Preheat oven to 475°F.

2. Spray pie pan with nonstick cooking spray. Place pie crust in prepared pan. Line pie crust with foil; fill with dried beans or rice. Bake 8 minutes. Remove foil and beans. Bake 4 minutes; set aside. *Reduce oven temperature to 375°F.*

3. Brown beef 6 to 8 minutes in large skillet over medium-high heat, stirring to break up meat. Drain fat. Add zucchini, mushrooms and green onions; cook and stir until tender. Add flour; cook and stir 2 minutes. Remove from heat.

4. Combine milk, cheese, eggs, thyme, salt, black pepper and red pepper in medium bowl. Stir into beef mixture; pour into crust. Bake 35 minutes or until knife inserted into center comes out clean. *Makes 6 servings*

Tamale Pie

Prep and Cook Time: 20 minutes

1 pound ground beef
1 can (about 14 ounces) diced tomatoes
1 package (10 ounces) frozen corn, thawed
1 can (4 ounces) sliced black olives, drained
1 package (1¼ ounces) taco seasoning mix
1 package (6 ounces) corn muffin mix, plus ingredients
    to prepare mix
¼ cup (1 ounce) shredded Cheddar cheese
1 green onion, thinly sliced

1. Preheat oven to 400°F. Brown beef 6 to 8 minutes in large skillet over medium-high heat, stirring to break up meat. Drain fat.

2. Add tomatoes, corn, olives and seasoning mix to beef; bring to a boil over medium-high heat, stirring constantly. Pour mixture into deep 9-inch pie plate; smooth top with spatula.

3. Prepare corn muffin mix according to package directions. Spread evenly over beef mixture. Bake 8 to 10 minutes or until golden brown. Sprinkle with cheese and green onion. Let stand 10 minutes before serving. *Makes 6 servings*

Tip: To meet USDA standards, all ground beef must be at least 70 percent lean. Ground sirloin and ground round are the leanest. Ground chuck contains more fat and therefore produces more juice. If you are not sure what to buy, ask your butcher.

Old-Fashioned Cabbage Rolls

8 ounces ground beef
8 ounces ground veal
8 ounces ground pork
1 onion, chopped
½ cup plain dry bread crumbs
2 eggs, lightly beaten
1 teaspoon *each* salt and molasses
¼ teaspoon *each* ground ginger, ground nutmeg and ground allspice
1 large head cabbage, separated into leaves
3 cups boiling water
¼ cup (½ stick) butter
½ cup milk, plus additional if necessary
1 tablespoon cornstarch

1. Combine beef, veal, pork and onion in large bowl. Combine bread crumbs, eggs, salt, molasses, ginger, nutmeg and allspice in medium bowl; mix well. Add to meat mixture; stir until well blended.

2. Boil cabbage leaves 3 minutes. Remove with slotted spoon; reserve ½ cup boiling liquid.

3. Preheat oven to 375°F. Place 2 tablespoons meat mixture about 1 inch from stem end of each cabbage leaf. Fold sides in and roll up, fastening with toothpicks, if necessary.

4. Heat butter in large skillet over medium-high heat. Add cabbage rolls, 3 or 4 at a time; brown on all sides. Arrange rolls, seam side down, in single layer in casserole. Combine reserved boiling liquid with butter remaining in skillet; pour over cabbage rolls.

5. Bake 1 hour. Carefully drain accumulated pan juices into measuring cup. Return cabbage rolls to oven.

6. Add enough milk to pan juices to equal 1 cup. Pour milk mixture into small saucepan. Whisk in cornstarch; bring to a boil, stirring constantly until sauce is thickened. Pour over cabbage rolls. Bake 15 minutes or until cabbage is tender. *Makes 8 servings*

Mini Meat Loaves & Vegetables

1½ **pounds lean ground beef**
1 **egg**
1 **can (8 ounces) tomato sauce, divided**
1⅓ **cups FRENCH'S® French Fried Onions, divided**
½ **teaspoon salt**
½ **teaspoon Italian seasoning**
6 **small red potatoes, thinly sliced (about 1½ cups)**
1 **bag (16 ounces) frozen vegetable combination (broccoli, corn, red bell pepper), thawed and drained**
Salt
Black pepper

1. Preheat oven to 375°F. In medium bowl, combine ground beef, egg, *½ can* tomato sauce, ⅔ *cup* French Fried Onions, ½ teaspoon salt and Italian seasoning. Shape into 3 mini loaves and place in 13×9-inch baking dish. Arrange potatoes around loaves.

2. Bake, covered, at 375°F for 35 minutes. Spoon vegetables around meat loaves; stir to combine with potatoes. Lightly season vegetables with salt and pepper, if desired. Top meat loaves with remaining tomato sauce. Bake, uncovered, 15 minutes or until meat loaves are done.

3. Top loaves with remaining ⅔ *cup* onions; bake, uncovered, 3 minutes or until onions are golden brown.   *Makes 6 servings*

Spicy Pork Chop Casserole

Prep Time: 15 minutes | Bake Time: 20 minutes

Nonstick cooking spray
2 cups frozen corn
2 cups frozen diced hash brown potatoes
1 can (about 14 ounces) diced tomatoes with basil,
garlic and oregano, drained
2 teaspoons chili powder
1 teaspoon dried oregano
½ teaspoon ground cumin
⅛ teaspoon red pepper flakes
1 teaspoon olive oil
4 boneless pork loin chops (about 3 ounces each), cut
about ¾ inch thick
¼ teaspoon black pepper
¼ cup (1 ounce) shredded Monterey Jack cheese (optional)

1. Preheat oven to 375°F. Lightly coat 8-inch square baking dish with cooking spray.

2. Lightly spray large nonstick skillet with cooking spray. Add corn; cook and stir over medium-high heat 5 minutes or until corn begins to brown. Add potatoes; cook and stir 5 minutes or until potatoes begin to brown. Add tomatoes, chili powder, oregano, cumin and red pepper flakes; stir until blended. Transfer to prepared baking dish.

3. Wipe out skillet with paper towel. Add oil; heat over medium-high heat. Add pork; cook until browned on one side. Place browned side up on top of corn mixture in baking dish. Sprinkle with black pepper.

4. Bake 20 minutes or until pork is barely pink in center. Sprinkle with cheese, if desired. Let stand 5 minutes before serving.

Makes 4 servings

Chicken and Turkey

Cajun Chicken and Rice

4 chicken drumsticks, skin removed
4 chicken thighs, skin removed
2 teaspoons Cajun seasoning
¾ teaspoon salt
2 tablespoons vegetable oil
1 can (about 14 ounces) chicken broth
1 cup uncooked rice
1 green bell pepper, coarsely chopped
1 red bell pepper, coarsely chopped
½ cup finely chopped green onions
2 cloves garlic, minced
½ teaspoon dried thyme
¼ teaspoon ground turmeric

1. Preheat oven to 350°F. Lightly coat 13×9-inch baking dish with nonstick cooking spray.

2. Pat chicken dry. Sprinkle both sides with Cajun seasoning and salt. Heat oil in large skillet over medium-high heat. Add chicken; cook 8 to 10 minutes or until browned on all sides. Transfer to plate.

3. Add broth to skillet. Bring to a boil, scraping up browned bits. Add rice, peppers, green onions, garlic, thyme and turmeric; stir well. Pour into prepared baking dish. Place chicken on top. Cover with foil. Bake 1 hour or until chicken is cooked through (165°F).

Makes 6 servings

Chili Wagon Wheel Casserole

8 ounces uncooked wagon wheel pasta
Nonstick cooking spray
1 pound ground turkey
¾ cup chopped onion
¾ cup chopped green bell pepper
1 can (about 14 ounces) stewed tomatoes, undrained
1 can (8 ounces) tomato sauce
½ teaspoon black pepper
¼ teaspoon ground allspice
½ cup (2 ounces) shredded Cheddar cheese

1. Preheat oven to 350°F. Cook pasta according to package directions until almost tender. Drain well.

2. Lightly coat large nonstick skillet with cooking spray; heat over medium-high heat. Add turkey; cook and stir 5 minutes or until no longer pink. Add onion and bell pepper; cook and stir until tender.

3. Stir in tomatoes with juice, tomato sauce, black pepper and allspice; cook 2 minutes. Stir in pasta. Spoon mixture into 2½-quart casserole. Sprinkle with cheese.

4. Bake 20 to 25 minutes or until heated through.

Makes 6 servings

Homestyle Chicken & Rice Casserole

Prep Time: 15 minutes | Cook Time: 60 minutes

1 cup long grain white rice
1 can (14 ounces) chicken broth
¾ cup chopped onion
2 cups small broccoli florets
4 (2½ pounds) bone-in chicken breast halves
1 teaspoon paprika
1 teaspoon thyme leaves
1 teaspoon garlic salt
2 cups (8 ounces) SARGENTO® Fancy Shredded Mild
   Cheddar Cheese

COMBINE rice, broth, onion and broccoli in 11×7-inch baking pan. Place chicken over rice mixture. Combine paprika, thyme and garlic salt in small bowl; sprinkle over chicken.

COVER with foil; bake in preheated 375°F oven 40 minutes. Uncover; bake 15 minutes more or until liquid is absorbed, rice is tender and chicken is cooked through.

SPRINKLE chicken and rice with cheese. Bake 5 minutes more or until cheese is melted.   *Makes 4 servings*

Tip: There are three commercial grades of rice: long, medium and short grain. The length of the rice kernel affects the texture of the cooked rice. Long grain rice kernels are four to five times longer than they are wide with tapered ends. They are lower in starch than shorter grained kernels, resulting in a less sticky finished product.

Chicken Chilaquiles

 12 (6- or 7-inch) corn tortillas
1½ to 2½ tablespoons vegetable oil, divided
 2 cups shredded cooked chicken
   Salsa
 6 eggs, beaten
 1 cup shredded queso Chihuahua or Manchego cheese
 ½ cup finely crumbled queso añejo or feta cheese
 ⅓ cup crema mexicana or crème fraîche

1. Preheat oven to 375°F. Spray 13×9-inch baking dish with nonstick cooking spray.

2. Place all tortillas in single stack on cutting board; cut into ¼- to ½-inch-wide strips. Heat 1½ teaspoons vegetable oil in large skillet over medium-high heat until shimmering. Add half the tortilla strips and fry until golden brown, gently stirring often to prevent tortilla strips from sticking to one another. Transfer with slotted spoon to prepared baking dish. Add remaining oil to skillet, if needed, and repeat with remaining tortilla strips.

3. Add chicken to baking dish. Pour salsa over tortilla strips and chicken; toss gently to coat evenly. Stir in eggs. Cover with foil.

4. Bake 35 minutes or until tortilla strips have absorbed enough sauce to become soft but not soggy and casserole is heated through. Remove foil and sprinkle with queso Chihuahua. Bake 5 to 10 minutes or until cheese is melted and casserole is lightly browned.

5. Remove from oven and cool slightly before serving. Sprinkle with crumbled queso añejo and drizzle with crema mexicana.

Makes 6 to 8 servings

Tip: Crema mexicana is a dairy product similar to sour cream or crème fraîche, either of which can be substituted if you are unable to find crema in your supermarket's dairy case. Crema mexicana is sweeter and creamier than crème fraîche, but it has a slightly bolder flavor than sour cream.

Chicken & Dumplings Casserole

¾ **pound chicken tenders, cut into bite-size pieces**
6 **baby potatoes, red or Yukon Gold, quartered**
 (about ½ pound)
1 **cup baby carrots**
1 **cup frozen green peas, thawed**
2 **tablespoons all-purpose flour**
¼ **teaspoon salt**
¼ **teaspoon black pepper**
1 **can (about 14 ounces) chicken broth**
½ **cup biscuit baking mix**
¼ **cup water**

1. Lightly coat 9-inch microwavable pie plate with cooking spray.

2. Place chicken, potatoes, carrots, peas, flour, salt and pepper in large resealable food storage bag. Seal bag and shake to coat chicken and vegetables with flour and seasonings. Empty chicken and vegetables into pie plate, shaking to distribute evenly. Add chicken broth. Cover with 10-inch circle of waxed paper and microwave on HIGH 20 minutes.

3. Combine biscuit mix and water in bowl; mix lightly with fork. Set aside.

4. Preheat oven to 400°F.

5. Remove pie plate from microwave. Remove and discard waxed paper. Drop teaspoons of biscuit dough over chicken and vegetables.

6. Bake in oven 10 minutes or until dumplings are puffed and cooked through. Remove from oven; let cool 5 minutes before serving. *Makes 6 servings*

Turkey and Rice Quiche

3 cups cooked rice, cooled to room temperature
1½ cups chopped cooked turkey
1 medium tomato, seeded and finely diced
¼ cup sliced green onions
¼ cup finely diced green bell pepper
1 tablespoon chopped fresh basil *or* 1 teaspoon
    dried basil leaves
½ teaspoon seasoned salt
⅛ to ¼ teaspoon ground red pepper
½ cup skim milk
3 eggs, beaten
   Vegetable cooking spray
½ cup (2 ounces) shredded Cheddar cheese
½ cup (2 ounces) shredded mozzarella cheese

Combine rice, turkey, tomato, green onions, bell pepper, basil, salt, red pepper, milk and eggs in 13×9×2-inch pan coated with cooking spray. Top with cheeses.

Bake at 375°F for 20 minutes or until knife inserted near center comes out clean. To serve, cut quiche into 8 squares; cut each square diagonally into 2 triangles.

Makes 8 servings (2 triangles each)

Favorite recipe from **USA Rice**

Chicken Penne Casserole

6 ounces penne pasta, uncooked
1 can (10¾ ounces) condensed cream of chicken soup,
    undiluted
1 cup chopped cooked chicken
1 cup (4 ounces) shredded sharp Cheddar cheese
½ cup sliced celery
½ cup milk
¼ cup mayonnaise
1 can (4 ounces) sliced water chestnuts, drained
1 jar (2 ounces) chopped pimientos, drained
½ teaspoon salt
    Dash black pepper
    Pinch celery seeds

1. Preheat oven to 350°F. Spray 2-quart casserole with nonstick cooking spray.

2. Cook pasta according to package directions; drain. Return to saucepan. Add soup, chicken, cheese, sliced celery, milk, mayonnaise, water chestnuts, pimientos, salt, pepper and celery seeds. Transfer to prepared casserole.

3. Bake 25 minutes or until bubbly and heated through.

Makes 6 servings

Turkey Pot Pie Casserole

Nonstick cooking spray
2 pounds turkey breast, cut into 1-inch cubes
¼ cup plus 2 tablespoons butter
⅓ cup all-purpose flour
½ teaspoon ground sage
½ teaspoon ground thyme
1½ cups chicken broth
1 cup milk
1 package (16 ounces) frozen soup vegetables (carrots, potatoes, peas, celery, green beans, corn, onions and lima beans)
1 teaspoon salt
½ teaspoon black pepper
1 can (8 ounces) refrigerated crescent roll dough

1. Preheat oven to 375°F. Spray 13×9-inch baking dish with cooking spray.

2. Spray large nonstick skillet with cooking spray; heat over medium heat. Working in batches, brown turkey on all sides. Transfer to large bowl.

3. Melt butter in skillet. Whisk in flour, sage and thyme; cook and stir 5 minutes. Slowly whisk in broth and milk; cook 5 minutes or until thickened, whisking constantly.

4. Stir in turkey, vegetables, salt and pepper; cook 5 to 7 minutes or until thick and creamy, stirring frequently. Spoon mixture into prepared baking dish. Unroll crescent roll dough; place over turkey mixture.

5. Bake 15 minutes or until golden brown.   *Makes 6 servings*

Creamy Chicken and Pasta with Spinach

6 ounces uncooked egg noodles
1 tablespoon olive oil
¼ cup chopped onion
¼ cup chopped red bell pepper
1 package (10 ounces) frozen spinach, thawed and drained
2 boneless skinless chicken breasts, cooked and cut into
      1-inch pieces
1 can (4 ounces) sliced mushrooms, drained
2 cups (8 ounces) shredded Swiss cheese
1 container (8 ounces) sour cream
¾ cup half-and-half
2 eggs, lightly beaten
½ teaspoon salt

1. Preheat oven to 350°F. Spray 13×9-inch baking dish with nonstick cooking spray. Cook noodles according to package directions; drain and set aside.

2. Heat oil in large skillet over medium-high heat. Add onion and bell pepper; cook and stir 2 minutes or until onion is tender. Add spinach, chicken, mushrooms and noodles; stir to blend.

3. Combine cheese, sour cream, half-and-half, eggs and salt in medium bowl; blend well. Add cheese mixture to chicken mixture; stir to blend. Transfer to prepared baking dish.

4. Bake, covered, 30 to 35 minutes or until heated through.

Makes 8 servings

Dairyland Confetti Chicken

1 cup diced carrots
¾ cup chopped onion
½ cup diced celery
¼ cup chicken broth
3 cups cubed cooked chicken
1 can (10½ ounces) cream of chicken soup, undiluted
1 cup dairy sour cream
½ cup (4 ounces) sliced mushrooms
1 teaspoon Worcestershire sauce
1 teaspoon salt
⅛ teaspoon black pepper
   Confetti Topping (recipe follows)
¼ cup (1 ounce) shredded Wisconsin Cheddar cheese

For casserole, in saucepan, combine carrots, onion, celery and
chicken broth. Simmer 20 minutes. In 3-quart casserole, mix cubed
chicken, soup, sour cream, mushrooms, Worcestershire sauce,
salt and pepper. Add simmered vegetables and liquid; mix well.
Prepare Confetti Topping. Drop tablespoons of Confetti Topping
onto casserole. Bake in 350°F oven for 40 to 45 minutes or until
golden brown. Sprinkle with cheese and return to oven until
melted. Garnish as desired.   *Makes 6 to 8 servings*

Confetti Topping

1 cup sifted all-purpose flour
2 teaspoons baking powder
½ teaspoon salt
2 eggs, lightly beaten
½ cup milk
1 tablespoon chopped green bell pepper
1 tablespoon chopped pimiento
1 cup (4 ounces) shredded Wisconsin Cheddar cheese

In mixing bowl, combine flour, baking powder and salt. Add eggs,
milk, green pepper, pimiento and cheese. Mix just until well
blended.   *Makes 2 cups*

Favorite recipe from Wisconsin Milk Marketing Board

Turnip Shepherd's Pie

1 pound turnips,* peeled and cut into ½-inch cubes
1 pound ground turkey
⅓ cup plain dry bread crumbs
¼ cup chopped onion
¼ cup ketchup
1 egg
   Salt and black pepper
½ teaspoon Beau Monde seasoning**
⅓ cup half-and-half
1 tablespoon butter or margarine
¼ cup (1 ounce) shredded sharp Cheddar cheese
1 tablespoon chopped fresh parsley

*For Rutabaga Shepherd's Pie, use 1 pound rutabagas in place of turnips.

**Beau Monde is a seasoning salt available in most supermarkets. Celery salt can be substituted.

1. Preheat oven to 400°F. Place turnips in large saucepan; cover with water. Cover and bring to a boil; reduce heat to medium-low. Simmer 20 minutes or until fork-tender.

2. Meanwhile, combine turkey, bread crumbs, onion, ketchup, egg, ½ teaspoon salt and ½ teaspoon pepper in large bowl; mix well. Pat onto bottom and up side of 9-inch pie pan. Bake 20 to 30 minutes or until turkey is no longer pink. Blot with paper towel to remove any drippings.

3. Drain turnips; mash until smooth. Add half-and-half and butter; stir until well blended. Season to taste with salt and black pepper. Fill meat shell with turnip mixture; sprinkle with cheese and parsley. Bake 5 minutes or until cheese is melted.

Makes 4 servings

Chicken-Asparagus Casserole

2 teaspoons vegetable oil
1 cup chopped green and/or red bell peppers
1 onion, chopped
2 cloves garlic, minced
1 can (10¾ ounces) condensed cream of asparagus soup,
　　undiluted
1 container (8 ounces) ricotta cheese
2 cups (8 ounces) shredded Cheddar cheese, divided
2 eggs
1½ cups chopped cooked chicken
1 package (10 ounces) frozen chopped asparagus,* thawed
　　and drained
8 ounces egg noodles, cooked
　　Black pepper (optional)

*Or substitute ½ pound fresh asparagus cut into ½-inch pieces. Bring
6 cups water to a boil over high heat in large saucepan. Add asparagus.
Reduce heat to medium. Cover and cook 5 to 8 minutes or until crisp-
tender. Drain.

1. Preheat oven to 350°F. Grease 13×9-inch casserole.

2. Heat oil in small skillet over medium heat. Add bell peppers,
onion and garlic; cook and stir until vegetables are crisp-tender.

3. Mix soup, ricotta cheese, 1 cup Cheddar cheese and eggs
in large bowl until well blended. Add onion mixture, chicken,
asparagus and noodles; mix well. Season with black pepper, if
desired. Spread mixture evenly in prepared casserole. Top with
remaining 1 cup Cheddar cheese.

4. Bake 30 minutes or until center is set and cheese is bubbly. Let
stand 5 minutes before serving. *Makes 12 servings*

Turkey & Green Bean Casserole

¼ cup slivered almonds, toasted*
1 package (7 ounces) herb stuffing mix
¾ cup chicken broth
1 can (about 10¾ ounces) condensed cream of mushroom
    soup, undiluted
¼ cup milk or half-and-half
¼ teaspoon black pepper
2 cups cubed cooked turkey or chicken
1 package (10 ounces) frozen French-style green beans,
    thawed and drained

*To toast almonds, spread in shallow baking pan. Bake in preheated
350°F oven 5 to 7 minutes or until fragrant, stirring occasionally.*

1. Preheat oven to 350°F. Spray 11×7-inch baking dish with
nonstick cooking spray.

2. Spread stuffing in prepared dish. Drizzle with broth; stir to
coat.

3. Combine soup, milk and pepper in large bowl. Add turkey
and green beans; stir until blended. Spoon over stuffing; top
with almonds.

4. Bake 30 to 35 minutes or until heated through.

Makes 4 servings

Barbecue Chicken with Corn Bread Topper

1½ pounds boneless skinless chicken breasts and thighs, cut into ¾-inch cubes
1 can (about 15 ounces) red beans, rinsed and drained
1 can (8 ounces) tomato sauce
1 cup chopped green bell pepper
½ cup barbecue sauce
1 package (6 ounces) corn bread mix, plus ingredients to prepare mix

1. Preheat oven to 375°F. Heat nonstick skillet over medium heat. Add chicken; cook and stir 5 minutes or until cooked through.

2. Combine chicken, beans, tomato sauce, bell pepper and barbecue sauce in microwavable 8-inch baking dish.

3. Loosely cover chicken mixture with plastic wrap. Microwave on MEDIUM-HIGH (70%) 8 minutes or until heated through, stirring after 4 minutes.

4. Meanwhile, prepare corn bread mix according to package directions. Spoon batter over chicken mixture.

5. Bake 15 to 18 minutes or until toothpick inserted into center of corn bread comes out clean. *Makes 8 servings*

Full of Beans

Red, White and Black Bean Casserole

2 tablespoons olive oil
1 yellow or green bell pepper, cut into ½-inch strips
½ cup sliced green onions
1 can (14½ ounces) chunky-style salsa
1 can (4½ ounces) green chiles, drained
1 package (1½ ounces) taco seasoning mix
2 tablespoons chopped fresh cilantro
½ teaspoon salt
2 cups cooked white rice
1 can (about 15 ounces) white cannellini beans, rinsed
   and drained
1 can (15 ounces) red kidney beans, rinsed and drained
1 can (15 ounces) black beans, rinsed and drained
1 cup (4 ounces) shredded Cheddar cheese, divided
1 package (6-inch) flour tortillas, warmed

1. Heat oil in large saucepan over medium-high heat. Add pepper
and green onions; cook and stir about 5 minutes. Add salsa,
chiles, taco seasoning, cilantro and salt; cook 5 minutes, stirring
occasionally. Stir in rice and beans. Remove from heat; stir in ½ cup
cheese.

2. Spoon mixture into prepared baking dish. Sprinkle remaining
½ cup cheese evenly over top. Cover and bake 30 to 40 minutes or
until heated through. Serve with warm tortillas.

Makes 6 servings

Chicken Cassoulet

4 slices bacon
¼ cup all-purpose flour
  Salt and black pepper
1¾ pounds bone-in chicken pieces
2 cooked chicken sausages (2¼ ounces each),
    cut into ¼-inch pieces
1 onion, chopped
1½ cups diced red and green bell peppers
2 cloves garlic, minced
1 teaspoon dried thyme
  Olive oil
2 cans (about 15 ounces each) cannellini or
    Great Northern beans, rinsed and drained
½ cup dry white wine (optional)

1. Preheat oven to 350°F. Cook bacon in large skillet over medium-high heat until crisp; drain on paper towels. Cut into 1-inch pieces.

2. Pour off all but 2 tablespoons fat from skillet. Combine flour, salt and black pepper in shallow bowl. Dip chicken pieces into flour mixture; shake off excess. Brown chicken in batches in skillet over medium-high heat; remove to plate. Lightly brown sausages in skillet; remove to plate.

3. Add onion, bell peppers, garlic and thyme to skillet. Cook and stir over medium heat 5 minutes or until softened, adding oil as needed to prevent sticking. Transfer onion mixture to 13×9-inch baking dish. Add beans; mix well. Top with chicken, sausages and bacon. Add wine to skillet, if desired; cook and stir over medium heat, stirring to scrape up browned bits. Pour over casserole.

4. Cover and bake 40 minutes. Uncover; bake 15 minutes or until chicken is cooked through (165°F). *Makes 6 servings*

Tex-Mex Bake

1 cup MINUTE® White or Brown Rice, uncooked
1 pound ground beef
1 can (15 ounces) chili beans
1 can (10 ounces) diced tomatoes with green chiles
1 bag (12 ounces) tortilla chips, crushed
1 pound prepared cheese product, cut into cubes, divided
Sliced green onions and sour cream (optional)

Preheat oven to 350°F. Prepare rice according to package directions; set aside.

Brown beef in large nonstick skillet over medium heat; drain excess fat. Mix in rice, beans and tomatoes with chiles.

Cover bottom of baking dish with chips. Layer half of cheese over chips. Top with rice mixture. Top with remaining cheese.

Bake, uncovered, 15 minutes or until cheese is melted. Garnish with green onions and sour cream, if desired.   *Makes 8 servings*

Carolina Baked Beans & Pork Chops

Prep Time: 10 minutes | Cook Time: 30 minutes

2 cans (16 ounces each) pork and beans
½ cup *each* chopped onion and chopped green bell pepper
¼ cup FRENCH'S® Classic Yellow® Mustard
¼ cup packed light brown sugar
2 tablespoons FRENCH'S® Worcestershire Sauce
1 tablespoon FRANK'S® REDHOT® Original Cayenne Pepper Sauce
6 boneless pork chops (1 inch thick)

1. Preheat oven to 400°F. Combine all ingredients *except pork chops* in 3-quart shallow baking dish; mix well. Arrange chops on top, turning once to coat with sauce.

2. Bake, uncovered, 30 to 35 minutes or until pork is no longer pink in center. Stir beans around chops once during baking. Serve with green beans or mashed potatoes, if desired.   *Makes 6 servings*

Oven Pork Cassoulet

Prep Time: 15 minutes | Bake Time: 35 to 40 minutes

1 tablespoon canola oil

1¼ pounds pork tenderloin, trimmed of fat and
    cut into 1-inch pieces

1 cup chopped onion

1 cup chopped carrots

3 cloves garlic, minced

2 cans (about 15 ounces each) cannellini beans,
    rinsed and drained

1 can (about 14 ounces) diced tomatoes with Italian
    seasoning

¼ pound smoked turkey sausage, cut into ¼-inch-thick
    slices

1 teaspoon dried thyme

¼ teaspoon salt

¼ teaspoon dried rosemary

¼ teaspoon black pepper

1. Preheat oven to 325°F. Heat oil in Dutch oven over medium heat; brown pork in batches. Transfer pork to plate with slotted spoon.

2. Add onion, carrots and garlic to Dutch oven; cook and stir 8 to 10 minutes or until tender.

3. Combine pork, onion mixture, beans, tomatoes, sausage, thyme, salt, rosemary and pepper in 3-quart casserole. Cover and bake 35 to 40 minutes or until pork is barely pink in center.

Makes 6 servings

Southwestern Lasagna

1 tablespoon vegetable oil
1 medium onion, thinly sliced
1 clove garlic, finely chopped
1 tablespoon chili powder
1 tablespoon paprika
¾ cup water
1 can (6 ounces) tomato paste
¼ cup honey
¼ cup fresh lime juice
1 can (15 ounces) black beans, undrained
1 can (12 ounces) whole kernel corn
6 medium corn tortillas, cut in quarters
1 package (15 ounces) part skim ricotta cheese
1 can (7 ounces) whole mild green chilies, cut lengthwise
    into ½-inch strips
½ cup (2 ounces) shredded Monterey Jack cheese

In medium saucepan, heat oil over medium-high heat until hot; cook and stir onions and garlic 3 to 5 minutes or until onion is tender. Add chili powder and paprika; cook and stir 1 minute. Stir in water, tomato paste, honey and lime juice until well mixed. Stir in black beans and corn. Bring to a boil; reduce heat and simmer 5 minutes.

Spoon ⅓ of sauce into 1½-quart rectangular baking pan; arrange ½ of tortilla quarters evenly over sauce in pan. Spread with ½ of ricotta cheese and arrange ½ of green chilies evenly over cheese. Repeat with ⅓ of sauce, remaining tortillas, ricotta cheese and green chilies. Spread remaining sauce evenly over top of lasagna; sprinkle evenly with shredded cheese. Bake at 350°F 20 to 25 minutes or until heated through. *Makes 6 servings*

Favorite recipe from National Honey Board

Vegetarian Paella

1 tablespoon olive oil
1 onion, chopped
1 serrano pepper,* finely chopped
1 red bell pepper, diced
1 green bell pepper, diced
3 cloves garlic, minced
½ teaspoon saffron threads
½ teaspoon paprika
1 cup long grain white rice
3 cups water
1 can (about 15 ounces) chickpeas, rinsed and drained
1 can (14 ounces) artichoke hearts in water, drained and
    cut into halves
1 cup frozen green peas
1½ teaspoons grated lemon peel
Fresh bay leaves (optional)
Lemon slices (optional)

*Serrano peppers can sting and irritate the skin, so wear rubber gloves
when handling peppers and do not touch your eyes.*

1. Preheat oven to 375°F.

2. Heat oil in heavy ovenproof skillet over medium heat. Add
onion, serrano pepper and bell peppers; cook and stir about
7 minutes.

3. Add garlic, saffron and paprika; cook 3 minutes. Add rice; cook
and stir 1 minute. Add water, chickpeas, artichoke hearts, peas and
lemon peel, mix well.

4. Cover; bake 25 minutes or until rice is tender. Garnish with bay
leaves and lemon slices.   *Makes 12 servings*

Beef, Bean and Pasta Casserole

2¾ cups uncooked whole wheat rigatoni pasta
1 pound ground beef
1 onion, diced
2 cloves garlic, minced
1 can (8 ounces) tomato sauce
1 can (about 15 ounces) cannellini beans, rinsed and
    drained
1 can (about 14 ounces) diced tomatoes, drained
2 teaspoons Italian seasoning
½ to ¾ teaspoon salt
¼ teaspoon black pepper
1 cup finely shredded Parmesan cheese
1 cup (4 ounces) shredded mozzarella cheese

1. Preheat oven to 350°F. Lightly spray 11×7-inch baking dish with nonstick cooking spray. Cook pasta according to package directions; drain.

2. Brown beef, onion and garlic 6 to 8 minutes in large skillet over medium-high heat, stirring to break up meat. Drain fat. Add tomato sauce, beans, tomatoes, Italian seasoning, salt and pepper; cook 3 minutes.

3. Remove skillet from heat; stir in pasta and Parmesan cheese. Transfer mixture to prepared dish; sprinkle with mozzarella cheese.

4. Bake 20 minutes or until casserole is bubbly and cheese is melted.

Makes 6 servings

Variations: Any short shaped pasta can be used in this recipe and/or red kidney beans can be used instead of the cannellini beans, if desired.

Family-Style Hot Dogs
with Rice and Red Beans

1 tablespoon vegetable oil

1 onion, chopped

½ green bell pepper, chopped

2 cloves garlic, minced

1 can (about 15 ounces) red kidney beans, rinsed and
  drained

1 can (about 15 ounces) Great Northern beans, rinsed and
  drained

½ pound beef hot dogs, cut into ¼-inch-thick pieces

1 cup uncooked instant brown rice

1 cup vegetable broth

¼ cup packed brown sugar

¼ cup ketchup

3 tablespoons dark molasses

1 tablespoon Dijon mustard

1. Preheat oven to 350°F. Lightly spray 13×9-inch baking dish with
nonstick cooking spray.

2. Heat oil in Dutch oven over medium-high heat. Add onion, bell
pepper and garlic; cook and stir 2 minutes or until tender.

3. Add beans, hot dogs, rice, broth, brown sugar, ketchup,
molasses and mustard; stir until blended. Transfer to prepared
baking dish. Cover with foil.

4. Bake 30 minutes or until rice is tender.   *Makes 6 servings*

Cajun-Style Beef and Beans

Prep Time: 35 minutes | Bake Time: 25 to 30 minutes | Stand Time: 5 minutes

1 pound ground beef
¾ cup chopped onion
2½ cups cooked brown rice
1 can (about 15 ounces) kidney beans, rinsed and drained
1 can (about 14 ounces) stewed tomatoes, undrained
2 teaspoons Cajun seasoning (recipe follows)
¾ cup (3 ounces) shredded Cheddar cheese

1. Preheat oven to 350°F.

2. Brown beef 6 to 8 minutes in large nonstick skillet over medium-high heat, stirring to break up meat. Drain fat. Add onion; cook and stir 2 minutes or until translucent. Combine beef mixture, rice, beans, tomatoes with juice and Cajun seasoning in 2- to 2½-quart casserole.

3. Cover and bake 25 to 30 minutes, stirring once. Sprinkle with cheese. Cover and let stand 5 minutes before serving.

Makes 6 servings

Cajun Seasoning

½ cup salt
¼ cup plus 1 tablespoon ground red pepper
3 tablespoons black pepper
3 tablespoons onion powder
3 tablespoons garlic powder
3 tablespoons chili powder
1 tablespoon dried thyme
1 tablespoon dried basil
1 tablespoon ground bay leaf

Combine salt, red pepper, black pepper, onion powder, garlic powder, chili powder, thyme, basil and ground bay leaf in medium bowl until well combined. Store in tightly sealed container.

Makes about 1¼ cups

Savory Lentil Casserole

1¼ cups dried brown or green lentils, rinsed and sorted
2 tablespoons olive oil
1 onion, chopped
3 cloves garlic, minced
8 ounces fresh shiitake or button mushrooms, sliced
2 tablespoons all-purpose flour
1½ cups beef broth
4 ounces Canadian bacon, minced
1 tablespoon Worcestershire sauce
1 tablespoon balsamic vinegar
½ teaspoon salt
½ teaspoon black pepper
½ cup grated Parmesan cheese
2 to 3 plum tomatoes, chopped

1. Preheat oven to 400°F. Grease 1½-quart casserole.

2. Place lentils in medium saucepan; add enough water to cover lentils. Bring to a boil over high heat. Reduce heat to low. Cover and simmer 20 to 25 minutes or until lentils are barely tender; drain.

3. Meanwhile, heat oil in large skillet over medium heat. Add onion and garlic; cook and stir 5 minutes. Add mushrooms; cook and stir 10 minutes or until liquid is evaporated and mushrooms are tender. Sprinkle flour over mushroom mixture; cook and stir 1 minute. Stir in broth, Canadian bacon, Worcestershire sauce, vinegar, salt and pepper; cook and stir until mixture is thick and bubbly. Stir in lentils. Spread evenly in prepared casserole. Sprinkle with cheese.

4. Bake 20 minutes. Sprinkle tomatoes over casserole just before serving. *Makes 4 servings*

Pasta & White Bean Casserole

    1 tablespoon olive oil
    ½ cup chopped onion
    2 cloves garlic, minced
    2 cans (about 15 ounces each) cannellini beans, rinsed
        and drained
    3 cups cooked small shell pasta
    1 can (about 8 ounces) tomato sauce
1½ teaspoons Italian seasoning
    ½ teaspoon salt
    ½ teaspoon black pepper
    1 cup (4 ounces) shredded Italian cheese blend
    2 tablespoons finely chopped fresh Italian parsley

1. Preheat oven to 350°F. Lightly coat 2-quart casserole with nonstick cooking spray.

2. Heat oil in large skillet over medium-high heat. Add onion and garlic; cook and stir 4 minutes or until onion is tender. Add beans, pasta, tomato sauce, Italian seasoning, salt and pepper; mix well. Transfer to prepared casserole; sprinkle with cheese and parsley.

3. Bake 20 minutes or until cheese is melted.

Makes 6 servings

Apple, Bean and Ham Casserole

Make-Ahead Time: up to 2 days in refrigerator | Final Cook Time: 15 minutes

**3 cans (15 ounces each) Great Northern beans,
   rinsed and drained**
1 pound boneless ham, cut into 1-inch cubes
1 Granny Smith apple, diced
1 onion, diced
3 tablespoons packed brown sugar
3 tablespoons dark molasses
1 tablespoon Dijon mustard
1 teaspoon ground allspice
⅓ cup water
**¼ cup thinly sliced green onions *or* 1 tablespoon
   chopped fresh parsley**

1. Preheat oven to 350°F. Combine beans, ham, apple, onion, brown sugar, molasses, mustard and allspice in 3-quart casserole; mix well.

2. Cover and bake 45 minutes or until most liquid is absorbed. Cool casserole completely. Cover and refrigerate up to 2 days.

3. Preheat oven to 350°F. Stir water into casserole.

4. Bake 40 minutes or until bubbly and heated through. Sprinkle with green onions before serving.   *Makes 6 servings*

Tip: Great Northern beans are large white beans that have a nutty flavor and dense texture. Great Northern beans are available both dried and canned.

Gourmet Bean & Spinach Burritos

Avocado Relish (page 169)
1 pound spinach leaves, divided
2 teaspoons olive oil
1 cup finely chopped onion
2 cloves garlic, minced
2 cans (about 15 ounces each) black beans, drained
1 can (10 ounces) whole tomatoes with green chiles, undrained
2 teaspoons ground cumin
½ teaspoon ground oregano
8 (8-inch) flour tortillas
2 cups (8 ounces) shredded Monterey Jack cheese
Sour cream (optional)

1. Prepare Avocado Relish. Remove and discard stems from spinach leaves. Set aside 24 to 30 large leaves. Stack remaining leaves and cut crosswise into ¼-inch-wide pieces. Set aside.

2. Heat oil in large nonstick skillet over medium heat. Add onion and garlic; cook and stir 5 minutes or until tender. Add beans, tomatoes with juice, cumin and oregano; simmer, uncovered, until mixture is dry. Remove from heat; mash bean mixture with potato masher.

3. Preheat oven to 350°F.

4. Arrange 3 to 4 whole spinach leaves on each tortilla. Spoon bean mixture onto bottom half of tortillas; sprinkle cheese evenly over bean mixture. Roll up to enclose filling. Arrange, seam sides down, in 12×8-inch baking dish. Cover with foil.

5. Bake 20 minutes or until heated through. To serve, arrange spinach pieces on each plate; top with burritos. Serve with sour cream and Avocado Relish. *Makes 4 servings*

Avocado Relish

1 large avocado, finely diced
2 tablespoons fresh lime juice
¾ cup finely chopped tomato
½ cup minced green onions
⅓ cup minced fresh cilantro
½ to 1 teaspoon hot pepper sauce

Combine avocado and lime juice in large bowl. Add tomato, green onions, cilantro and hot pepper sauce; toss gently. Cover and refrigerate 1 hour. Serve at room temperature.

Makes about 2¼ cups

Southwestern Tortilla Stack

1 can (about 30 ounces) vegetarian refried beans
½ cup sour cream
1 can (4 ounces) mild chopped green chiles, drained
½ teaspoon ground cumin
3 (10-inch) flour tortillas
1 cup (4 ounces) shredded Cheddar cheese
Salsa (optional)

1. Preheat oven to 425°F. Grease 10-inch round casserole dish.

2. Combine beans, sour cream, chiles and cumin in medium bowl.

3. Place one tortilla in bottom of prepared casserole. Top with half of bean mixture and one third of cheese. Top with second tortilla; repeat layers of beans and one third of cheese.

4. Cover with remaining tortilla; sprinkle with remaining cheese.

5. Cover and bake 20 minutes or until heated through. Cut into wedges. Serve with salsa, if desired. *Makes 4 to 6 servings*

Vegetable Sides

Barley Vegetable Casserole

2¼ **cups vegetable broth, divided**
⅔ **cup uncooked barley (not quick-cooking)**
4 **cups frozen mixed vegetables (broccoli, cauliflower,**
   carrots and onions)
½ **teaspoon garlic powder**
¼ **teaspoon black pepper**
½ **teaspoon butter**
½ **teaspoon salt**

1. Preheat oven to 350°F. Spray 1-quart casserole with nonstick cooking spray.

2. Place ¼ cup broth and barley in nonstick skillet; cook over medium heat 3 minutes or until lightly browned, stirring frequently. Transfer to prepared casserole.

3. Add vegetables, garlic powder, pepper and remaining 2 cups broth to casserole; mix well.

4. Cover and bake 50 minutes or until barley is tender and most liquid is absorbed, stirring several times. Stir in butter and salt. Let stand 5 minutes before serving.   *Makes 4 servings*

Fruited Corn Pudding

5 cups thawed frozen corn, divided
5 eggs
½ cup milk
1½ cups whipping cream
⅓ cup unsalted butter, melted and cooled
1 teaspoon vanilla
½ teaspoon salt
¼ teaspoon ground nutmeg
3 tablespoons finely chopped dried apricots
3 tablespoons dried cranberries or raisins
3 tablespoons finely chopped dates
2 tablespoons finely chopped dried pears or
    other dried fruit

1. Preheat oven to 350°F. Grease 13×9-inch baking dish.

2. Combine 3½ cups corn, eggs and milk in food processor or blender; process until almost smooth.

3. Transfer corn mixture to large bowl. Add cream, butter, vanilla, salt and nutmeg; stir until well blended. Add remaining 1½ cups corn, apricots, cranberries, dates and pears; stir well. Pour mixture into prepared baking dish.

4. Bake 50 to 60 minutes or until center is set and top begins to brown. Let stand 10 to 15 minutes before serving.

Makes 8 servings

Apple & Carrot Casserole

6 carrots, sliced
4 apples, peeled and sliced
¼ cup plus 1 tablespoon all-purpose flour
1 tablespoon packed brown sugar
½ teaspoon ground nutmeg
1 tablespoon butter
½ cup orange juice
½ teaspoon salt

1. Preheat oven to 350°F. Cook carrots in boiling water in large saucepan 5 minutes; drain. Layer carrots and apples in large casserole.

2. Combine flour, brown sugar and nutmeg in small bowl; sprinkle over top. Dot with butter; pour orange juice over casserole. Sprinkle with salt. Bake 30 minutes or until carrots are tender.

Makes 6 servings

Festive Sweet Potato Combo

Prep Time: 10 minutes | Cook Time: 38 minutes

2 cans (16 ounces each) sweet potatoes, drained
1⅓ cups FRENCH'S® French Fried Onions, divided
1 large apple, sliced into thin wedges
2 cans (8 ounces each) crushed pineapple, undrained
3 tablespoons packed light brown sugar
¾ teaspoon ground cinnamon

1. Preheat oven to 375°F. Grease 2-quart shallow baking dish. Layer sweet potatoes, ⅔ *cup* French Fried Onions and half of the apple wedges in prepared baking dish.

2. Stir together pineapple with liquid, sugar and cinnamon in medium bowl. Spoon pineapple mixture over sweet potato mixture. Arrange remaining apple wedges over pineapple layer.

3. Cover; bake 35 minutes or until heated through. Uncover; sprinkle with remaining ⅔ *cup* onions. Bake 3 minutes or until onions are golden. *Makes 6 servings*

Broccoli & Cheddar Noodle Casserole

Prep Time: 25 minutes | Cook Time: 25 minutes

1 package (12 ounces) dry wide egg noodles
3 tablespoons margarine or butter, divided
2 cups chopped onions
4 cups broccoli flowerets
1 can (14½ ounces) CONTADINA® Stewed Tomatoes with
   onions, celery & green peppers, undrained
1 can (6 ounces) CONTADINA Tomato Paste
1 package (1½ ounces) spaghetti sauce seasoning mix
2 cups water
1 teaspoon garlic salt
1½ cups (6 ounces) shredded Cheddar cheese
½ cup CONTADINA Seasoned Italian Bread Crumbs

1. Cook noodles according to package directions; drain.

2. Meanwhile, melt 2 tablespoons margarine in 5-quart saucepan; sauté onions until tender.

3. Stir in broccoli, undrained tomatoes, tomato paste, seasoning mix, water and garlic salt. Bring to a boil. Reduce heat; simmer, uncovered, for 10 minutes, stirring occasionally. Stir in cooked noodles.

4. Layer half of noodle mixture in 13×9×2-inch baking dish. Sprinkle with cheese. Layer with remaining noodle mixture.

5. Melt remaining 1 tablespoon margarine; stir in crumbs. Sprinkle over casserole; cover and bake in preheated 350°F oven 20 minutes. Uncover; bake 5 minutes.   *Makes 6 servings*

Herbed Cauliflower Casserole

5 cups cauliflower florets (about 1¼ pounds)
1 tablespoon butter, melted
1 red bell pepper, cut into quarters
2 tablespoons water
3 tomatoes, peeled and coarsely chopped
2 to 3 teaspoons chopped fresh tarragon
½ teaspoon chopped fresh parsley
⅓ cup (about 9 to 10) coarsely crushed saltine crackers

1. Preheat oven to 450°F.

2. Toss cauliflower with butter in large bowl. Place cauliflower and bell pepper, cut sides down, in single layer in shallow baking pan; add water. Roast vegetables 15 minutes. *Reduce oven temperature to 425°F.*

3. Roast 25 to 28 minutes until cauliflower is tender and golden brown and bell pepper skin is blistered. Remove bell pepper to plate and transfer cauliflower to 11×7-inch baking dish. *Reduce oven temperature to 400°F.*

4. Place tomatoes in food processor or blender. Remove and discard skin from bell pepper.

5. Add bell pepper to food processor or blender; process until smooth. Add tarragon and parsley; process until blended. Pour tomato sauce over cauliflower.

6. Bake 10 minutes or until casserole is bubbly and heated through. Sprinkle with cracker crumbs just before serving.

Makes 5 servings

Corn Pudding

1 tablespoon butter
1 onion, chopped
1 tablespoon all-purpose flour
2 cups half-and-half
1 cup milk
¼ cup quick-cooking grits or polenta
2 cups corn
1 can (4 ounces) diced mild green chiles, drained
¾ teaspoon salt
¼ teaspoon black pepper
¼ teaspoon hot pepper sauce
4 eggs, lightly beaten

1. Preheat oven to 325°F. Grease 11×7-inch baking dish.

2. Melt butter in large saucepan over medium heat. Add onion; cook and stir 5 minutes or until tender and golden. Stir in flour; cook until golden. Stir in half-and-half and milk; bring to a boil. Whisk in grits; reduce heat to medium-low. Cook and stir 10 minutes or until mixture is thickened.

3. Remove from heat. Stir in corn, chiles, salt, black pepper and hot pepper sauce. Stir in eggs. Pour into prepared baking dish.

4. Bake 1 hour or until knife inserted into center comes out clean.

Makes 8 servings

Scalloped Apples & Onions

1 medium onion, thinly sliced
4 tablespoons butter, melted, divided
5 red or green apples, cored and thinly sliced
8 ounces (1½ cups) pasteurized process cheese, cut into
    small pieces, divided
2 cups FRENCH'S® French Fried Onions, divided

1. Preheat oven to 375°F. Sauté onion in 2 tablespoons butter in medium skillet over medium-high heat 3 minutes or until tender. Add apples and sauté 5 minutes or until apples are tender.

2. Stir 1 cup cheese, *1 cup* French Fried Onions and remaining melted butter into apple mixture. Transfer to greased 9-inch deep-dish pie plate.

3. Bake, uncovered, 20 minutes or until heated through. Top with remaining cheese and onions. Bake 5 minutes or until cheese is melted. *Makes 6 side-dish servings*

Tip: To save time and cleanup, apple mixture may be baked in a heatproof skillet, if desired. Wrap skillet handle in heavy-duty foil.

Saucy Vegetable Casserole

Prep Time: 5 minutes | Cook Time: 20 minutes

**2 bags (16 ounces each) frozen mixed vegetables
(broccoli, cauliflower, carrots), thawed
2 cups FRENCH'S® French Fried Onions, divided
1 package (16 ounces) pasteurized process cheese,
cut into ¼-inch slices**

1. Preheat oven to 350°F. Combine vegetables and *1 cup* French Fried Onions in shallow 3-quart baking dish. Top evenly with cheese slices.

2. Bake 15 minutes or until hot and cheese is almost melted; stir. Top with remaining *1 cup* onions and bake 5 minutes or until onions are golden. *Makes 8 servings*

Tip: For added Cheddar flavor, substitute French's® Cheddar French Fried Onions for the original flavor.

Fresh Vegetable Casserole

8 **new potatoes**
8 **baby carrots**
1 **head cauliflower, broken into florets**
4 **stalks asparagus, cut into 1-inch pieces**
3 **tablespoons butter**
3 **tablespoons all-purpose flour**
2 **cups milk**
   Salt and black pepper
¾ **cup (3 ounces) shredded Cheddar cheese**
   Chopped fresh cilantro or parsley

1. Preheat oven to 350°F. Grease 2-quart casserole.

2. Steam potatoes, carrots, cauliflower and asparagus until crisp-tender. Arrange vegetables in prepared casserole.

3. Melt butter in medium saucepan over medium heat. Stir in flour until smooth. Gradually whisk in milk; bring to a boil. Cook and stir 2 minutes or until thick and bubbly. Season with salt and pepper. Add cheese, stirring until melted. Pour sauce over vegetables and sprinkle with cilantro.

4. Bake 15 minutes or until heated through.

Makes 4 to 6 servings

Horseradish Scalloped Potatoes

¾ **cup milk**

3 **tablespoons horseradish**

2 **pounds Yukon Gold potatoes, peeled and cut into**
   ¼-inch-thick slices

¾ **cup whipping cream**

1 **teaspoon salt**

½ **teaspoon black pepper**

½ **cup (2 ounces) shredded Swiss cheese**

1. Preheat oven to 375°F. Grease 1½-quart casserole.

2. Combine milk and horseradish in medium microwavable bowl. Microwave on HIGH 1 minute or just until heated through.

3. Layer potato slices in prepared casserole. Stir cream, salt and pepper into milk mixture; pour over potatoes.

4. Cover and bake 40 minutes. Sprinkle with cheese; bake, uncovered, 40 minutes or until bubbly and golden brown.

Makes 4 to 6 servings

Southwest Spaghetti Squash

1 spaghetti squash (about 3 pounds)
1 can (about 14 ounces) Mexican-style diced tomatoes
1 can (about 14 ounces) black beans, rinsed and drained
¾ cup (3 ounces) shredded Monterey Jack cheese, divided
¼ cup finely chopped fresh cilantro
1 teaspoon ground cumin
¼ teaspoon garlic salt
¼ teaspoon black pepper

1. Preheat oven to 350°F. Spray baking sheet and 1½-quart baking dish with nonstick cooking spray. Cut squash in half lengthwise. Remove and discard seeds. Place squash, cut side down, on prepared baking sheet.

2. Bake 45 minutes or just until tender. Shred hot squash with fork; place flesh in large bowl.

3. Add tomatoes, beans, ½ cup cheese, cilantro, cumin, garlic salt and pepper; toss well. Spoon mixture into prepared baking dish. Sprinkle with remaining ¼ cup cheese.

4. Bake 30 to 35 minutes or until heated through. Serve immediately.
Makes 4 servings

Tip: Spaghetti squash, which weighs from three to five pounds, is oblong with creamy yellow skin and pale yellow flesh. It gets its name because the flesh separates into spaghetti-like strands when cooked.

Acorn Squash with
Corn Bread Stuffing

1 acorn squash (about 2 pounds)
¼ cup (½ stick) butter, divided
2 cups chopped mushrooms
1 onion, chopped
1 stalk celery, chopped
¾ cup seasoned corn bread stuffing mix
¼ teaspoon salt
¼ teaspoon black pepper
2 tablespoons packed brown sugar, divided

1. Preheat oven to 375°F. Cut squash into quarters; remove and discard seeds. Place squash, skin side up, in microwavable dish; add ½ inch water to dish. Cover loosely with plastic wrap.

2. Microwave on HIGH 8 to 10 minutes or until tender.* Drain well.

3. Meanwhile, melt 2 tablespoons butter in large saucepan over medium heat. Add mushrooms, onion and celery; cook and stir 7 to 10 minutes or until tender. Remove from heat. Stir in stuffing mix, salt and pepper.

4. Place squash in baking dish, cut side up. Top each quarter with remaining 1½ teaspoons butter and 1½ teaspoons brown sugar. Pack ½ cup stuffing onto each quarter.

5. Bake 25 to 30 minutes or until stuffing is golden brown.

Makes 4 servings

To cook on stovetop, place squash quarters in large saucepan with boiling water to cover. Cook 30 minutes or until fork-tender. Drain well.

Saucy Garden Patch Vegetables

1 can (10¾ ounces) condensed Cheddar cheese soup
½ cup sour cream
¼ cup milk
1 bag (16 ounces) frozen vegetable combination, such
    as broccoli, corn and red bell pepper, thawed and
    drained
1 bag (16 ounces) frozen vegetable combination, such as
    brussels sprouts, carrots and cauliflower, thawed and
    drained
1 cup (4 ounces) shredded Cheddar cheese
1⅓ cups FRENCH'S® French Fried Onions, divided

Microwave Directions

1. Combine soup, sour cream and milk in large bowl. Stir in
vegetables, cheese and ⅔ *cup* French Fried Onions. Spoon into
microwavable 2-quart oblong baking dish.

2. Cover loosely with plastic wrap. Microwave on HIGH 10 minutes
or until vegetables are tender and mixture is heated through,
stirring halfway through cooking time.

3. Uncover; sprinkle with remaining ⅔ *cup* onions. Microwave on
HIGH 1 minute or until onions are golden.

Makes 8 to 10 servings

Oven Directions: Prepare vegetable mixture as above. Bake,
covered, in 400°F oven 45 minutes or until tender and mixture
is heated through. Stir; sprinkle with remaining onions. Bake,
uncovered, 1 minute.

Pies

Table of Contents

Banana Cream Pie

 1 unbaked 9-inch pie crust
 3 bananas, divided
 1 teaspoon lemon juice
 ½ cup sugar
 ¼ cup plus 2 tablespoons cornstarch
 ¼ teaspoon salt
 3 cups milk
 2 egg yolks
 1½ teaspoons vanilla
     Whipped cream (optional)
     Ground cinnamon (optional)

1. Preheat oven to 400°F. Prick holes in bottom of crust with fork. Bake 10 minutes or until lightly browned. Cool 15 minutes on wire rack.

2. Slice 2 bananas; toss with lemon juice. Layer on bottom of crust.

3. Combine sugar, cornstarch and salt in medium saucepan. Combine milk and egg yolks in medium bowl; slowly stir into sugar mixture. Cook and stir over medium heat until thickened. Boil 1 minute, stirring constantly. Remove from heat; stir in vanilla. Pour into crust; cover with waxed paper. Refrigerate 2 hours or until ready to serve.

4. Remove waxed paper and slice remaining banana. Arrange slices around edge of pie. Garnish with whipped cream and cinnamon.

Makes 8 servings

CARNATION® Key Lime Pie

1 can (14 ounces) NESTLÉ® CARNATION® Sweetened Condensed Milk
½ cup (about 3 medium limes) fresh lime juice
1 teaspoon grated lime peel
1 *prepared* 9-inch (6 ounces) graham cracker crumb crust
2 cups frozen whipped topping, thawed
 Lime peel twists or lime slices (optional)

BEAT sweetened condensed milk and lime juice in small mixer bowl until combined; stir in lime peel. Pour into crust; spread with whipped topping. Refrigerate for 2 hours or until set. Garnish with lime peel twists.

Makes 8 servings

Mom's Pumpkin Pie

1½ cans (15 ounces each) solid-pack pumpkin
1 can (12 ounces) evaporated milk
1 cup sugar
2 eggs
2 tablespoons maple syrup
1 teaspoon ground cinnamon
1 teaspoon vanilla
½ teaspoon salt
2 unbaked 9-inch pie crusts
 Whipped cream (optional)

1. Preheat oven to 350°F.

2. Combine pumpkin, evaporated milk, sugar, eggs, maple syrup, cinnamon, vanilla and salt in large bowl. Spread evenly into crusts. Place pie pans on baking sheet.

3. Bake 1 hour or until knife inserted into centers comes out clean. Cool completely on wire rack. Serve with whipped cream, if desired.

Makes 16 servings

CARNATION® Key Lime Pie

Boston Cream Pie

1 cup granulated sugar
⅓ cup shortening
1 egg
1 teaspoon vanilla
1¼ cups all-purpose flour
1½ teaspoons baking powder
½ teaspoon salt
¾ cup milk
    Cream Filling (recipe follows)
    Chocolate Glaze (recipe follows)

1. Preheat oven to 350°F. Grease and flour 9-inch round cake pan.

2. Beat 1 cup granulated sugar and shortening in large bowl with lelectric mixer at medium speed until light and fluffy. Blend in egg and vanilla. Combine flour, baking powder and salt in medium bowl. Add flour mixture to sugar mixture alternately with milk, beating well after each addition. Pour into prepared pan.

3. Bake 35 minutes or until toothpick inserted into center comes out clean. Cool in pan 10 minutes.

4. Meanwhile, prepare Cream Filling. Loosen edge of cake and remove to wire rack to cool completely. Prepare Chocolate Glaze. Split cake in half horizontally. Spoon Cream Filling over bottom half of cake; cover with top half. Spread top with Chocolate Glaze. Refrigerate. Serve when glaze is completely set.

Makes 8 servings

Cream Filling: Combine ⅓ cup granulated sugar, 2 tablespoons cornstarch and ¼ teaspoon salt in medium saucepan. Stir in 1½ cups milk; cook over medium heat, stirring constantly, until mixture thickens and comes to a boil. Boil 1 minute, stirring constantly. Stir small amount of hot mixture into 2 slightly beaten egg yolks in small bowl; mix thoroughly. Return to saucepan. Bring to a boil; boil 1 minute, stirring constantly. *Do not overcook.* Remove from heat; stir in 2 teaspoons vanilla. Refrigerate until cooled completely.

Chocolate Glaze: Combine 2 (1-ounce) squares unsweetened chocolate and 3 tablespoons butter in medium saucepan; cook and stir over low heat until melted. Remove from heat. Stir in 1 cup sifted powdered sugar and 1 teaspoon vanilla. Stir in 3 to 5 teaspoons water, 1 teaspoon at a time, until glaze is desired consistency. Cool slightly.

Boston Cream Pie

Strawberry Rhubarb Pie

Double-Crust Pie Pastry (recipe follows)
1½ cups sugar
½ cup cornstarch
2 tablespoons quick-cooking tapioca
1 tablespoon grated lemon peel
¼ teaspoon ground allspice
4 cups sliced (1-inch pieces) rhubarb
3 cups sliced strawberries
1 egg, lightly beaten

1. Preheat oven to 425°F. Roll out one disc of pastry into 11-inch circle on lightly floured surface. Line 9-inch pie plate with pastry.

2. Combine sugar, cornstarch, tapioca, lemon peel and allspice in large bowl. Add rhubarb and strawberries; toss to coat. Pour into crust. (Do not mound in center.)

3. Roll out remaining disc of pastry into 10-inch circle. Cut into ½-inch-wide strips. Arrange in lattice design over fruit; seal and flute edge. Brush pastry with egg.

4. Bake 50 minutes or until crust is golden brown and filling is thick and bubbly. Cool on wire rack. *Makes 8 servings*

Double-Crust Pie Pastry

2½ cups all-purpose flour
1 teaspoon salt
1 teaspoon sugar
1 cup (2 sticks) unsalted butter, cubed
⅓ cup water

1. Combine flour, salt and sugar in large bowl. Cut in butter using pastry blender or two knives until mixture resembles coarse crumbs.

2. Drizzle water over flour mixture, 2 tablespoons at a time, stirring just until dough comes together. Divide dough into two discs. Wrap in plastic wrap and refrigerate 30 minutes. *Makes 2 pastries*

Strawberry Rhubarb Pie

Classic Apple Pie

1 package (15 ounces) refrigerated pie crusts
6 cups sliced Granny Smith, Crispin or other firm-fleshed
    apples (about 6 medium)
½ cup sugar
1 tablespoon cornstarch
2 teaspoons lemon juice
½ teaspoon ground cinnamon
½ teaspoon vanilla
⅛ teaspoon salt
⅛ teaspoon ground nutmeg
⅛ teaspoon ground cloves
1 tablespoon whipping cream

1. Let crusts stand at room temperature 15 minutes. Preheat oven to 350°F. Line 9-inch pie plate with one crust.

2. Combine apples, sugar, cornstarch, lemon juice, cinnamon, vanilla, salt, nutmeg and cloves in large bowl. Pour into crust. Place second crust over apples; seal and flute edge. Cut four slits in top crust; brush with cream.

3. Bake 40 minutes or until crust is golden brown. Cool completely on wire rack.
Makes 8 servings

Fruit pies can be covered and stored at room
temperature overnight; refrigerate them
3 to 4 days for longer storage.

Classic Apple Pie

Lemon-Lime Meringue Pie

1 unbaked deep-dish 9-inch pie crust
4 eggs, separated
¾ cup plus 1 tablespoon sugar, divided
⅛ teaspoon salt
½ cup whipping cream
1 tablespoon cornstarch
3 tablespoons lemon juice
3 tablespoons lime juice
2 teaspoons grated lemon peel
2 teaspoons grated lime peel
2 tablespoons unsalted butter, cut into small pieces

1. Preheat oven to 400°F. Prick holes in bottom of crust with fork. Bake 10 minutes or until light brown. Cool completely on wire rack.

2. *Reduce oven temperature to 325°F.* Whisk egg yolks, ½ cup plus 1 tablespoon sugar and salt in medium saucepan until blended. Whisk cream and cornstarch in small bowl until smooth. Stir into egg yolk mixture.

3. Stir in lemon juice, lime juice, lemon peel and lime peel; cook and stir over medium heat until thickened. Remove from heat; stir in butter until melted. Pour into crust.

4. Beat egg whites in medium bowl with electric mixer at medium speed until frothy. Add remaining ¼ cup sugar, 1 tablespoon at a time, beating at high speed after each addition until stiff and glossy. Gently spread meringue over filling.

5. Bake 20 minutes or until meringue is golden brown. Cool completely on wire rack.   *Makes 12 servings*

Lemon-Lime Meringue Pie

Country Pecan Pie

Single-Crust Pie Pastry (page 264)
1¼ cups dark corn syrup
4 eggs
½ cup packed light brown sugar
¼ cup (½ stick) butter or margarine, melted
2 teaspoons all-purpose flour
1½ teaspoons vanilla
1½ cups pecan halves

1. Preheat oven to 350°F. Roll pastry on lightly floured surface to form 13-inch circle. Fit into 9-inch pie plate. Trim edges; flute. Set aside.

2. Beat corn syrup, eggs, brown sugar and butter in large bowl with electric mixer at medium speed 2 to 3 minutes or until well blended. Stir in flour and vanilla until blended. Pour into unbaked pastry. Arrange pecans on top.

3. Bake 40 to 45 minutes or until center of filling is puffed and golden brown. Cool completely on wire rack. *Makes 8 servings*

Favorite Peanut Butter Pie

¾ cup creamy peanut butter, divided
1 (6-ounce) shortbread cookie crumb pie crust
½ cup peanut butter chips, divided
1 package (3 ounces) cream cheese, softened
1 cup powdered sugar
1 container (8 ounces) frozen nondairy whipped topping, thawed

1. Spread ¼ cup peanut butter over bottom of crust. Sprinkle with ¼ cup peanut butter chips.

2. Beat cream cheese and sugar in medium bowl with electric mixer at low speed; beat in remaining ½ cup peanut butter until light and fluffy. Fold in whipped topping.

3. Pour into crust and sprinkle with remaining ¼ cup peanut butter chips. Serve immediately or refrigerate. *Makes 8 servings*

Country Pecan Pie

Dole® Very Peachy Pie

¾ cup sugar
3½ tablespoons minute tapioca
¼ teaspoon salt
6 cups DOLE® Frozen Sliced Peaches, thawed
1 tablespoon lemon juice
¼ teaspoon grated lemon peel
   Pastry for 9-inch double-crust pie
2 tablespoons butter or margarine, cut into small pieces
   Milk

• Combine sugar, tapioca and salt in small bowl.

• Combine peaches, lemon juice, lemon peel and sugar mixture in large bowl; mix well.

• Roll out half of pastry and fit into pie pan. Roll out remaining pastry.

• Spoon peach mixture into pie pan. Dot with butter. Top with remaining pastry; trim, turn under and flute edges.

• Cut a few slits in top. Brush lightly with milk and sprinkle with additional sugar, if desired.

• Lightly cover edges with thin strips of aluminum foil. Bake at 425°F 20 minutes. Remove foil and bake 20 to 25 minutes longer or until golden brown. Cool on wire rack.   *Makes 8 servings*

Prep Time: 20 minutes
Bake Time: 45 minutes

Dole® Very Peachy Pie

Fourth of July Cherry Pie

5 cups pitted Northwest fresh sweet cherries
2 tablespoons cornstarch
    Pastry for 2-crust (9-inch) pie
2 tablespoons butter or margarine
⅓ cup sifted powdered sugar
1 tablespoon fresh lemon juice
1 teaspoon grated lemon peel

Preheat oven to 425°F.

Sprinkle cornstarch over cherries; toss to coat. Turn into pastry-lined 9-inch pie pan. Dot with butter. Roll remaining pastry into 10-inch circle. Cut into ¾-inch-wide strips. Arrange lattice-fashion over filling; seal and flute edges. Bake 35 to 45 minutes or until filling bubbles. Combine powdered sugar, lemon juice and peel; drizzle over warm pie.   *Makes one 9-inch pie*

Combination Method: Preheat oven to 425°F. Prepare pie as above in microwave/ovenproof pie plate. Microwave at HIGH 10 minutes or until filling bubbles; remove to conventional oven and bake 10 to 15 minutes or until crust is golden.

Favorite recipe from **Northwest Cherry Growers**

A pie pan or plate is exclusively designed for baking a pie. A pie pan is a metal utensil; pie plate generally refers to a glass or ceramic utensil. Both are round, about 1¾ inches deep and have sloping sides. They range in diameter from 8 to 12 inches, with 9 inches being the most popular size. Glass or dark metal pie pans produce a crisp, golden brown crust. Shiny aluminum pans produce a paler crust.

Fourth of July Cherry Pie

Lemon Meringue Pie

1 unbaked 9-inch pie crust

Filling

1½ cups water
1 cup sugar
⅓ cup cornstarch
¼ teaspoon salt
4 egg yolks
½ cup fresh lemon juice (3 to 4 lemons)
2 tablespoons grated lemon peel
2 tablespoons butter

Meringue

8 tablespoons sugar, divided
⅓ cup water
1 tablespoon cornstarch
½ teaspoon vanilla
4 egg whites
¼ teaspoon cream of tartar

1. Preheat oven to 350°F. Prick holes in bottom of crust with fork. Bake 10 minutes or until lightly browned. Cool 15 minutes on wire rack.

2. For filling, mix 1½ cups water, 1 cup sugar, ⅓ cup cornstarch and salt in large saucepan. Bring to a simmer over medium heat; cook until mixture becomes thick and translucent. Quickly whisk in egg yolks. Add lemon juice, lemon peel and butter; return to a simmer. Cook 1 minute. Remove from heat. Pour hot filling into crust. Cover surface of filling with plastic wrap to keep hot and prevent skin from forming. Set aside.

3. For meringue, mix 1 tablespoon sugar, ⅓ cup water, 1 tablespoon cornstarch and vanilla in small saucepan. Bring to a boil; boil 1 minute. Remove from heat. Cool. Beat egg whites in medium bowl with electric mixer at high speed until frothy. Combine remaining 7 tablespoons sugar and cream of tartar in small bowl; beat into egg whites in two batches until soft peaks form. Add cornstarch mixture, 1 tablespoon at a time; beat until stiff peaks form. Immediately spread meringue onto filling.

4. Bake 12 to 15 minutes or until the peaks of meringue are golden brown. Let cool before serving. *Makes 8 servings*

Lemon Meringue Pie

Amaretto Coconut Cream Pie

1 container (8 ounces) whipped topping, divided
1 container (8 ounces) coconut cream yogurt or vanilla yogurt
¼ cup amaretto liqueur
1 package (4-serving size) coconut instant pudding and pie filling mix
1 (6-ounce) graham cracker pie crust
¼ cup flaked coconut*
  Fresh strawberries and mint leaves (optional)

*To toast coconut, cook and stir coconut in small skillet over medium heat 3 to 4 minutes or until light golden brown.

1. Combine 2 cups whipped topping, yogurt and amaretto in large bowl. Add pudding mix; whisk 2 minutes or until thickened.

2. Spread pudding mixture evenly in crust; spread remaining whipped topping over filling. Sprinkle with toasted coconut. Garnish with strawberries and mint. Refrigerate until serving.   *Makes 8 servings*

Custard Pie

  Pastry for single crust 9-inch pie
4 eggs, lightly beaten
½ cup sugar
¼ teaspoon salt
2½ cups milk, scalded (heated to just below boiling point)
2 teaspoons WATKINS® Vanilla
⅛ teaspoon WATKINS® Almond Extract
¼ teaspoon WATKINS® Nutmeg

Preheat oven to 400°F. Place pastry in pie pan and chill while preparing filling. Blend eggs, sugar and salt in large bowl. Gradually stir in scalded milk. Add extracts; stir until blended. Pour into pastry-lined pie pan; sprinkle with nutmeg. Bake for 25 to 30 minutes or until knife inserted halfway between outside and center comes out clean. Cool on wire rack for 30 minutes; refrigerate until completely chilled.   *Makes 10 servings*

Amaretto Coconut Cream Pie

Grasshopper Pie

2 cups graham cracker crumbs
¼ cup unsweetened cocoa powder
¼ cup (½ stick) butter, melted
1 package (8 ounces) cream cheese, softened
¼ cup sugar
1 cup milk
1½ teaspoons vanilla
1 teaspoon mint extract
4 to 6 drops green food coloring (optional)
1 container (8 ounces) whipped topping, thawed

1. Spray 9-inch pie plate with nonstick cooking spray. Combine cracker crumbs, cocoa and butter in medium bowl. Press onto bottom and up side of prepared pie plate. Refrigerate.

2. Beat cream cheese and sugar in large bowl with electric mixer at medium speed until fluffy. Gradually beat in milk until smooth. Stir in vanilla, mint extract and food coloring, if desired. Fold in whipped topping. Refrigerate 20 minutes or until chilled but not set. Pour into crust.

3. Freeze 4 hours or until set. Let stand at room temperature 10 minutes before serving.

Makes 8 servings

Chocolate Peanut Butter Pie

1 can (14 ounces) sweetened condensed milk
¼ cup creamy peanut butter
2 tablespoons unsweetened cocoa powder
1 container (8 ounces) thawed whipped topping, plus additional
    for topping
1 (6-ounce) chocolate crumb pie crust

1. Beat sweetened condensed milk, peanut butter and cocoa in large bowl with electric mixer at medium speed until smooth and well blended. Fold in whipped topping. Pour into crust.

2. Freeze at least 6 hours or overnight. Let stand at room temperature 10 minutes before serving. Top each serving with additional whipped topping. *Makes 8 servings*

Banana Split Pie

2 small ripe bananas
1 Ready-Crust Pie Crust KEEBLER® READY CRUST® Chocolate
1 quart vanilla ice cream, softened
1 cup frozen non-dairy whipped topping, thawed
½ cup hot fudge ice cream topping
⅓ cup pineapple ice cream topping
¼ cup chopped pecans, walnuts or peanuts
8 maraschino cherries

1. Slice bananas into crust. Spread ice cream over bananas. Freeze at least 4 hours or until firm.

2. Let stand at room temperature for 15 minutes before cutting. Serve pieces topped with whipped topping, fudge topping, pineapple topping, nuts and cherries. *Makes 8 servings*

Prep Time: 5 minutes
Freeze Time: 4 hours

Chocolate Peanut Butter Pie

Frozen Marble Swirl Pie

15 OREO® Cookies, crushed (about 1½ cups crumbs)
3 tablespoons butter, melted
1 tub (8 ounces) COOL WHIP® Whipped Topping, thawed, divided
1 cup cold 2% milk
1 package (4-serving size) JELL-O® Vanilla Flavor Instant Pudding & Pie Filling
2 squares BAKER'S® Semi-Sweet Baking Chocolate, melted
⅓ cup canned sweetened condensed milk
Maraschino cherries, optional

Mix cookie crumbs and butter; press firmly onto bottom and up side of 9-inch pie plate. Set aside. Remove ½ cup of the whipped topping; store in refrigerator until ready to use.

Pour 2% milk into large bowl. Add dry pudding mix. Beat with wire whisk 2 minutes or until well blended. Gently stir in remaining whipped topping. Spoon into crust. Mix melted chocolate and condensed milk until well blended. Drop in spoonfuls over pie; cut through chocolate mixture several times with knife for marble effect.

Freeze 6 hours or overnight until firm. Remove from freezer about 15 minutes before serving. Let stand at room temperature to soften slightly. Top with reserved ½ cup whipped topping. Garnish with maraschino cherry, if desired. Store leftover pie in freezer. *Makes 10 servings*

Pistachio Ice Cream Pie

1 jar (12 ounces) hot fudge dessert topping, divided
1 (6-ounce) chocolate crumb pie crust
4 cups pistachio ice cream, softened
½ cup chopped pistachios

1. Spread half of hot fudge topping over bottom of crust; freeze 10 minutes. Spread ice cream evenly over fudge topping. Sprinkle with chopped pistachios. Cover.

2. Freeze 2 hours or until firm. Let stand at room temperature 10 minutes before serving. Warm remaining fudge topping according to package directions; serve with pie. *Makes 8 servings*

Frozen Marble Swirl Pie

Easy Cherry Cream Pie

  1 pint vanilla ice cream, softened
½ (16-ounce) package frozen dark sweet cherries, chopped
  1 cup whipping cream
  1 tablespoon powdered sugar
⅛ teaspoon almond extract
  1 (6-ounce) chocolate crumb or graham cracker pie crust

1. Combine ice cream and cherries in large bowl just until blended. Beat cream, sugar and almond extract in medium bowl with electric mixer at medium speed until soft peaks form. Spread ice cream evenly in crust. Spoon whipped cream evenly on top.

2. Freeze 1 hour or until firm. Let stand at room temperature 10 minutes before serving. *Makes 8 servings*

Prep Time: 10 minutes

Chocolate Peaches & Cream Pie

  ½ cup chocolate syrup
  1 Ready-Crust Pie Crust KEEBLER® READY CRUST® Shortbread
  1 quart peach or vanilla ice cream, softened
12 fresh or canned peach slices, drained
  ¼ cup pecan halves, toasted*
    Additional chocolate syrup for garnish

*To toast pecans, spread evenly on baking sheet. Bake at 350°F for 5 to 10 minutes or until light golden brown, stirring once or twice.

1. Spread ½ cup chocolate syrup in crust. Spoon ice cream on top of syrup. Freeze at least 3 hours or until firm.

2. Let stand 15 minutes at room temperature before cutting. Top with peach slices and pecan halves. Drizzle with additional chocolate syrup.
Makes 8 servings

Prep Time: 10 minutes
Freeze Time: 3 hours

Easy Cherry Cream Pie

Frozen Margarita Pie

Crust
  10 ORTEGA® Yellow Corn Taco Shells
  ½ cup (1 stick) butter
  ½ cup granulated sugar

Filling
  1 can (14 ounces) sweetened condensed milk
  ⅓ cup frozen limeade, thawed
  2 tablespoons orange juice
  1 drop green food coloring
  1 cup whipping cream
  Lime curls (optional)

PLACE taco shells in food processor and pulse until evenly ground.

MELT butter in medium saucepan over low heat. Remove from heat. Stir in taco crumbs and sugar until well blended. Press firmly over bottom and up sides of 9-inch pie plate. Place in freezer until firm.

COMBINE sweetened condensed milk, limeade, orange juice and food coloring in large mixing bowl.

WHIP cream until soft peaks form. Fold whipped cream gently into condensed milk mixture until blended. Pour into prepared crust.

FREEZE, uncovered, 4 hours or until firm. Let stand 10 minutes before serving. Garnish with lime curls, if desired.   *Makes 8 servings*

Tip: To crush taco shells without a food processor, place them in a resealable plastic food storage bag and run a rolling pin over the shells until they are evenly crushed.

Prep Time: 15 minutes
Start to Finish: 4 hours

Chocolate Mudslide Frozen Pie

1 cup (6 ounces) NESTLÉ® TOLL HOUSE® Semi-Sweet
    Chocolate Morsels
1 teaspoon NESCAFÉ® TASTER'S CHOICE® 100% Pure Instant
    Coffee Granules
1 teaspoon hot water
¾ cup sour cream
½ cup granulated sugar
1 teaspoon vanilla extract
1 *prepared* 9-inch (6 ounces) chocolate crumb crust
1½ cups heavy whipping cream
1 cup powdered sugar
¼ cup NESTLÉ® TOLL HOUSE® Baking Cocoa
2 tablespoons NESTLÉ® TOLL HOUSE® Semi-Sweet Chocolate
    Mini Morsels

MELT *1 cup* morsels in small, *heavy-duty* saucepan over *lowest possible* heat. When morsels begin to melt, remove from heat; stir. Return to heat for a few seconds at a time, stirring until smooth. Remove from heat; cool for 10 minutes.

COMBINE coffee granules and water in medium bowl. Add sour cream, granulated sugar and vanilla extract; stir until sugar is dissolved. Stir in melted chocolate until smooth. Spread into crust; refrigerate.

BEAT cream, powdered sugar and cocoa in small mixer bowl until stiff peaks form. Spread or pipe over chocolate layer. Sprinkle with mini morsels. Freeze for at least 6 hours or until firm.   *Makes 8 servings*

Pumpkin Ice Cream Pie
with Caramel Sauce

25 gingersnap cookies, finely crushed (about 1½ cups)
¼ cup (½ stick) unsalted butter, melted
2 tablespoons granulated sugar
1 quart pumpkin ice cream, softened
1 cup packed dark brown sugar
½ cup whipping cream
¼ cup plus 2 tablespoons (¾ stick) unsalted butter, cubed
¼ cup light corn syrup
½ teaspoon salt
1 cup chopped pecans, toasted*

To toast pecans, spread in single layer on baking sheet. Bake in preheated 350°F oven 8 to 10 minutes or until golden brown, stirring frequently. Cool.

1. Preheat oven to 350°F. Spray 9-inch pie plate with nonstick cooking spray.

2. Combine cookie crumbs, melted butter and granulated sugar in medium bowl. Press onto bottom and up side of prepared pie plate. Bake 8 minutes. Cool completely on wire rack.

3. Spread ice cream evenly in crust. Cover and freeze 1 hour.

4. Whisk brown sugar, cream, cubed butter, corn syrup and salt in medium saucepan over medium-high heat until sugar is dissolved. Boil 1 minute without stirring. Cool completely. Drizzle brown sugar mixture evenly over pie; sprinkle with pecans.   *Makes 8 servings*

Peppermint Ice Cream Pie

4 cups vanilla ice cream
6 peppermint candies plus additional for garnish
1 (6-ounce) graham cracker pie crust
Chocolate syrup

1. Scoop ice cream into medium bowl; let stand at room temperature 5 minutes or until softened, stirring occasionally.

2. Place 6 candies in small resealable food storage bag; coarsely crush with rolling pin or meat mallet. Stir candy into ice cream; spread evenly in crust. Cover.

3. Freeze at least 4 hours or overnight. Let stand at room temperature 10 minutes before serving. Drizzle each serving with chocolate syrup. Garnish with additional candies.

Makes 8 servings

Brownie Bottom Ice Cream Pie

1 package (about 16 ounces) refrigerated brownie batter
5 to 6 cups fudge ripple, cookies and cream or any flavor ice cream, softened
1 jar (8 ounces) hot fudge dessert topping

1. Preheat oven to 350°F. Spray 9-inch pie pan with nonstick cooking spray. Let batter stand at room temperature 5 minutes to soften.

2. Place batter in prepared pan; use dampened hands to spread batter over bottom and halfway up side of pan. Bake 20 minutes or until toothpick inserted into center comes out clean. Cool completely in pan on wire rack. Top brownie layer with ice cream, spreading to edge.

3. Serve immediately or cover with plastic wrap and freeze up to several hours. (If frozen, let pie stand at room temperature 10 minutes before serving.) Drizzle with hot fudge before serving. *Makes 8 servings*

Serving Suggestions: Serve the pie with additional toppings such as whipped cream, chopped nuts, sprinkles and maraschino cherries.

Peppermint Ice Cream Pie

Fudge-Bottomed Chocolate Layer Pie

1 cup HERSHEY®S SPECIAL DARK® Chocolate Chips, divided
2 tablespoons plus ¼ cup milk, divided
1 packaged chocolate crumb crust (6 ounces)
1½ cups miniature marshmallows
1 container (8 ounces) frozen non-dairy whipped topping, thawed and
    divided
    Additional sweetened whipped cream or whipped topping (optional)

1. Place ⅓ cup chocolate chips and 2 tablespoons milk in microwave-safe bowl. Microwave 30 seconds at MEDIUM (50%); stir. If necessary, microwave an additional 15 seconds at a time, stirring after each heating, until chips are melted and mixture is smooth when stirred. Spread on bottom of crust. Refrigerate while preparing next step.

2. Place marshmallows, remaining ⅔ cup chocolate chips and remaining ¼ cup milk in small saucepan. Cook over medium heat, stirring constantly, until marshmallows are melted and mixture is well blended. Transfer to separate large bowl; cool completely.

3. Stir 2 cups whipped topping into cooled chocolate mixture; spread 2 cups mixture over chocolate in crust. Blend remaining whipped topping and remaining chocolate mixture; spread over surface of pie.

4. Cover; freeze several hours or until firm. Garnish as desired. Cover and freeze leftover pie.   *Makes 6 to 8 servings*

Fudge-Bottomed Chocolate Layer Pie

Frozen Lemonade Pie

1 cup graham cracker crumbs (about 7½ crackers crushed)
1 cup plus 2 tablespoons sugar, divided
1 tablespoon butter, melted
1 tablespoon canola oil
1 egg white
2 cups plain yogurt
1 cup thawed whipped topping
6 tablespoons lemon juice (2 lemons)
 Grated peel of 1 lemon
½ teaspoon lemon extract
2 to 3 drops yellow food coloring (optional)
 Peel of 1 lemon, cut into thin strips (optional)

1. Preheat oven to 350°F. Spray 9-inch pie pan with nonstick cooking spray.

2. Process graham cracker crumbs, 2 tablespoons sugar, butter and oil in food processor or blender. Add egg white; process until well blended. Press crumb mixture onto bottom and up side of prepared pie plate.

3. Bake 8 to 10 minutes. Cool completely on wire rack.

4. Combine remaining 1 cup sugar, yogurt, whipped topping, lemon juice, grated lemon peel, lemon extract and food coloring, if desired. Pour into cooled crust; smooth top. Lightly cover with plastic wrap.

5. Freeze 4 hours or until firm. Let stand at room temperature 10 minutes before serving. Garnish with lemon peel strips.   *Makes 8 servings*

Frozen Lemonade Pie

Peanut Butter Cup Cookie Ice Cream Pie

½ cup creamy peanut butter
¼ cup honey
1 cup Cookies KEEBLER® Chips Deluxe™ Peanut Butter Cups
   (about 8 cookies)
1 quart vanilla ice cream, softened
1 Ready-Crust Pie Crust KEEBLER® READY CRUST® Chocolate
½ cup chocolate ice cream topping

1. Place large bowl in freezer.

2. In small bowl stir together peanut butter and honey. Set aside. Coarsely chop cookies.

3. In chilled bowl combine ice cream, peanut butter mixture and cookies. Beat on low speed of electric mixer until combined. Spread half of ice cream mixture in crust. Drizzle with ice cream topping. Carefully spread remaining ice cream mixture on top.

4. Freeze at least 3 hours or until firm. Let stand at room temperature for 15 minutes before cutting. Garnish as desired. Store in freezer.

Makes 8 servings

Prep Time: 15 minutes
Freeze Time: 3 hours

Chocolate Cookie Pie

20 chocolate sandwich cookies
1 cup whipping cream
1 (6-ounce) chocolate crumb pie crust

1. Place 14 cookies in large resealable food storage bag and crush into coarse crumbs. Beat cream in large bowl with electric mixer at high speed until soft peaks form. Stir crumbs into whipped cream; spread evenly in crust. Garnish with remaining cookies. Cover.

2. Freeze until ready to serve. Let stand at room temperature 10 minutes before serving.

Makes 8 servings

Peanut Butter Cup Cookie Ice Cream Pie

Crunchy Ice Cream Pie

1 (8-ounce) chocolate bar, chopped
2 tablespoons butter
1½ cups crisp rice cereal
½ gallon chocolate chip or fudge ripple ice cream, softened
    Hot fudge dessert topping

1. Spray 9-inch pie plate with nonstick cooking spray.

2. Combine chocolate and butter in top of double boiler over simmering water; cook and stir until chocolate is melted. Remove from heat. Add cereal; stir to coat. Transfer to prepared pie plate; press to form crust. Spread ice cream evenly in crust. Cover.

3. Freeze 2 hours or until firm. Let stand at room temperature 10 minutes before serving. Drizzle with hot fudge topping.   *Makes 8 servings*

Strawberry Sundae Pie

¼ cup creamy peanut butter
3 tablespoons corn syrup
2 cups crisp rice cereal
1¾ cups chocolate frozen yogurt, slightly softened
1½ cups strawberry or raspberry sorbet
    Sliced fresh strawberries (optional)

1. Spray 9-inch pie plate with nonstick cooking spray. Combine peanut butter and corn syrup in medium bowl; stir until blended. Stir in cereal until coated. Press onto bottom and up side of prepared pie plate. Loosely cover and refrigerate 15 minutes.

2. Gently spread frozen yogurt in crust. Use small ice cream scoop to scoop sorbet into small balls onto yogurt layer. Cover.

3. Freeze 2 hours or until firm. Let stand at room temperature 10 minutes before serving. Garnish with sliced strawberries.   *Makes 8 servings*

Crunchy Ice Cream Pie

Chocolate Caramel Surprise Pie

1½ cups plus 6 tablespoons whipping cream, divided
8 ounces semisweet chocolate, chopped, divided
1 (6-ounce) chocolate crumb pie crust
¼ cup caramel dessert topping
6 tablespoons sugar, divided
¼ teaspoon salt
3 egg yolks
½ teaspoon vanilla
   Whipped topping and caramels (optional)

1. Cook and stir ½ cup whipping cream and 4 ounces chocolate in small heavy saucepan over low heat until chocolate is melted; cool slightly. Spread evenly in crust. Refrigerate 30 minutes.

2. Spread dessert topping over chocolate. Refrigerate 30 minutes.

3. Cook and stir 1 cup whipping cream and remaining 4 ounces chocolate in same saucepan over low heat until chocolate is melted. Stir in 4 tablespoons sugar and salt; cool slightly.

4. Whisk egg yolks in small bowl. Pour ½ cup chocolate mixture into egg yolks, whisking constantly. Pour egg mixture back into saucepan; cook and stir over low heat until mixture is thickened. Cook 1 minute. (Mixture should reach 160°F on instant-read thermometer.) Transfer to large bowl; stir in vanilla. Refrigerate 30 minutes, stirring occasionally.

5. Beat remaining 6 tablespoons whipping cream and 2 tablespoons sugar in small bowl with electric mixer at high speed until stiff peaks form; fold into chocolate mixture. Gently spoon over caramel layer. Refrigerate 4 hours or overnight. Serve with whipped topping and caramels, if desired.

Makes 8 servings

Chocolate & Banana Cream Layered Pie

Graham Cracker Crust (recipe follows)
3 tablespoons cornstarch
½ teaspoon salt
1 cup cold water
1 can (14 ounces) sweetened condensed milk
4 egg yolks, beaten
⅓ cup plus 1 tablespoon half-and-half, divided
1 tablespoon unsalted butter
1½ teaspoons vanilla
1 square (1 ounce) unsweetened chocolate, finely chopped
2 bananas, divided
½ cup thawed whipped topping plus additional for topping
Grated semisweet chocolate (optional)

1. Prepare Graham Cracker Crust.

2. Combine cornstarch and salt in medium saucepan. Stir in water until cornstarch dissolves. Stir in sweetened condensed milk, egg yolks and ⅓ cup half-and-half; bring to a boil over medium heat. Cook about 8 minutes, stirring constantly. Remove from heat; stir in butter and vanilla.

3. Measure out 1 cup hot filling and place in small bowl. Stir in chocolate and remaining 1 tablespoon half-and-half until blended. Cool slightly, then spread chocolate filling on bottom of crust. Refrigerate 1 hour. Transfer vanilla filling to medium bowl; cover with plastic wrap and refrigerate 1 hour.

4. Cut one banana crosswise into ¼-inch slices; arrange over chocolate filling. Fold ½ cup whipped topping into vanilla filling; spoon filling over banana slices. Cover with plastic wrap and refrigerate at least 3 hours.

5. Spread pie with additional whipped topping. Slice remaining banana; garnish pie with banana slices and grated chocolate.

Makes 8 servings

Graham Cracker Crust: Preheat oven to 375°F. Combine 1¼ cups graham cracker crumbs, ⅓ cup melted unsalted butter and 3 tablespoons sugar in medium bowl. Mix with fork until blended. Press mixture onto bottom and up side of 9-inch pie pan. Bake 7 to 8 minutes. Cool completely on wire rack.

Chocolate Mint Cookie Pie

30 marshmallows
½ cup milk
4 ounces bittersweet chocolate, finely chopped
2 ounces unsweetened chocolate, finely chopped
½ teaspoon mint extract
1½ cups whipping cream
1 (6-ounce) chocolate crumb pie crust
1 container (8 ounces) whipped topping, thawed
12 chocolate mint sandwich cookies, chopped

1. Combine marshmallows and milk in medium saucepan; cook over medium heat 7 minutes or until melted and smooth, stirring constantly. Remove from heat. Stir in chocolate and mint extract until chocolate is melted and smooth.

2. Beat cream in medium bowl with electric mixer at high speed until stiff peaks form. Fold one fourth of whipped cream into chocolate mixture just until blended. Fold chocolate mixture into remaining whipped cream until blended. Spread evenly in crust. Spread whipped topping over top. Sprinkle with cookie pieces.

3. Refrigerate at least 3 hours or overnight. *Makes 8 servings*

Fancy Fudge Pie

1 cup chocolate wafer crumbs
⅓ cup butter, melted
1⅓ cups (8 ounces) semisweet chocolate chips
¾ cup packed brown sugar
½ cup (1 stick) butter, softened
3 eggs
1 cup chopped pecans
½ cup all-purpose flour
1 teaspoon vanilla
½ teaspoon instant espresso powder
　Whipped cream (optional)
　Chocolate syrup (optional)

1. Preheat oven to 375°F. Combine wafer crumbs and melted butter in small bowl. Press onto bottom and up side of 9-inch pie pan. Bake 5 minutes. Cool completely on wire rack.

2. Place chocolate chips in small microwavable bowl. Microwave on HIGH 1 minute or until melted and smooth. Cool slightly.

3. Beat sugar and softened butter in large bowl with electric mixer at medium speed until light and fluffy. Add eggs, one at a time, beating well after each addition. Stir in chocolate, pecans, flour, vanilla and espresso powder. Pour into crust.

4. Bake 30 minutes or until set. Cool completely on wire rack. Cover and refrigerate 2 hours or until ready to serve. Garnish with whipped cream and chocolate syrup. *Makes 8 servings*

Fancy Fudge Pie

Chocolate & Peanut Pie

1½ cups all-purpose flour
½ cup plus 1 tablespoon sugar, divided
½ teaspoon salt, divided
½ cup (1 stick) unsalted butter, melted
¾ cup half-and-half
½ cup semisweet chocolate chips
3 eggs
½ teaspoon vanilla
½ cup caramel dessert topping
¾ cup honey-roasted peanuts

1. Preheat oven to 425°F. Combine flour, 1 tablespoon sugar and ¼ teaspoon salt in medium bowl. Slowly pour in butter, stirring until dough forms.

2. Transfer dough to 9-inch pie pan; press on bottom and up side of pan, forming high rim. Place on baking sheet. Bake 5 minutes. Remove from oven. *Reduce oven temperature to 350°F.*

3. Combine half-and-half and chocolate chips in top of double boiler over simmering water. Cook until chocolate is melted, stirring occasionally. Remove from heat; stir in remaining ½ cup sugar and ¼ teaspoon salt. Beat in eggs, one at a time, until blended. Stir in vanilla.

4. Spread dessert topping evenly over bottom of crust; sprinkle with peanuts. Gently spoon chocolate mixture into crust. (Most peanuts will float to top.) Let stand until set.

5. Bake 45 minutes or until set. Cool 15 minutes on wire rack. Refrigerate at least 4 hours or overnight. *Makes 8 servings*

Creamy Milk Chocolate Pudding Pie

⅔ cup sugar
6 tablespoons cornstarch
2 tablespoons HERSHEY®S Cocoa
½ teaspoon salt
3 cups milk
4 egg yolks
2 tablespoons butter or margarine, softened
1 tablespoon vanilla extract
5 HERSHEY®S Milk Chocolate bars (1.55 ounces each), broken into
    pieces
1 packaged chocolate crumb crust (6 ounces)
    Sweetened whipped cream or whipped topping
    Additional HERSHEY®S Milk Chocolate Bar (1.55 ounces), cut into
    sections along score lines (optional)

1. Stir together sugar, cornstarch, cocoa and salt in 2-quart saucepan. Combine milk and egg yolks in bowl or container with pouring spout. Gradually blend milk mixture into sugar mixture.

2. Cook over medium heat, stirring constantly, until mixture comes to a boil. Boil and stir 1 minute. Remove from heat; stir in butter and vanilla. Add chocolate bar pieces; stir until bars are melted and mixture is well blended. Pour into crumb crust; press plastic wrap onto filling. Cool.

3. Refrigerate several hours or until chilled and firm. Remove plastic wrap. Garnish with whipped cream and chocolate bar sections. Cover; refrigerate leftovers.   *Makes 6 to 8 servings*

Creamy Milk Chocolate Pudding Pie

Chocolate Velvet Pie

1 unbaked deep-dish 9-inch pie crust
4 ounces semisweet chocolate
¾ cup half-and-half
3 eggs, divided
1 egg yolk
½ cup plus 2 tablespoons sugar, divided
1 teaspoon vanilla, divided
⅛ teaspoon salt
1 package (8 ounces) cream cheese, softened
¼ cup whipping cream
Raspberries and semisweet chocolate curls (optional)

1. Preheat oven to 400°F. Prick holes in bottom of crust with fork. Bake 10 minutes or until light brown. Cool completely on wire rack. *Reduce oven temperature to 350°F.*

2. Combine chocolate and half-and-half in medium heavy saucepan over medium-low heat; cook and stir until chocolate is melted. Remove from heat.

3. Beat 2 eggs and egg yolk in small bowl with electric mixer at low speed until blended. Beat into chocolate mixture. Beat in 6 tablespoons sugar, ½ teaspoon vanilla and salt until well blended. Spread evenly in crust.

4. Beat cream cheese and remaining 4 tablespoons sugar in medium bowl at medium-high speed until smooth. Beat in cream, remaining egg and ½ teaspoon vanilla until well blended. Gently drop cream cheese mixture by spoonfuls over filling to cover surface of pie.

5. Bake 40 minutes or until set. Cool completely on wire rack. Cover and refrigerate at least 2 hours before serving. Garnish with raspberries and chocolate curls. *Makes 12 servings*

Chocolate Velvet Pie

NESTLÉ® TOLL HOUSE®
Chocolate Chip Pie

2 large eggs
½ cup all-purpose flour
½ cup granulated sugar
½ cup packed brown sugar
¾ cup (1½ sticks) butter, softened
1 cup (6 ounces) NESTLÉ® TOLL HOUSE® Semi-Sweet Chocolate Morsels
1 cup chopped nuts
1 *unbaked* 9-inch (4-cup volume) deep-dish pie shell*
Sweetened whipped cream or ice cream (optional)

*If using frozen pie shell, use deep-dish style, thawed completely. Bake on baking sheet; increase baking time slightly.

PREHEAT oven to 325°F.

BEAT eggs in large mixer bowl on high speed until foamy. Beat in flour, granulated sugar and brown sugar. Beat in butter. Stir in morsels and nuts. Spoon into pie shell.

BAKE for 55 to 60 minutes or until knife inserted halfway between outside edge and center comes out clean. Cool on wire rack. Serve warm with whipped cream.   *Makes 8 servings*

Granny's No-Crust Chocolate Pie

½ cup plus 3 tablespoons granulated sugar, divided
3 tablespoons all-purpose flour
3 tablespoons unsweetened cocoa powder
⅛ teaspoon salt
2 cups milk
3 eggs, separated
2 tablespoons butter
1 teaspoon vanilla

1. Grease 9-inch pie pan.

2. Combine ½ cup sugar, flour, cocoa and salt in medium saucepan. Gradually whisk in milk and egg yolks; cook and stir over low heat until smooth and thickened. Remove from heat; stir in butter and vanilla. Pour into prepared pan; refrigerate 1 hour or until set.

3. Preheat oven to 400°F.

4. Beat egg whites in medium bowl with electric mixer at high speed until foamy. Add remaining 3 tablespoons sugar; beat until stiff peaks form. Spread pie with meringue.

5. Bake 8 to 10 minutes or until meringue is golden brown. Cool on wire rack 15 minutes.   *Makes 8 servings*

Gimme S'more Pie

1 can (12 fluid ounces) NESTLÉ® CARNATION® Evaporated Milk, *divided*
1 package (3.4 ounces) chocolate instant pudding and pie filling mix
1 (6 ounces) *prepared* 9-inch graham cracker crumb crust
3 cups mini marshmallows, *divided*
2 cups frozen whipped topping, thawed
½ cup NESTLÉ® TOLL HOUSE® Milk Chocolate Morsels

WHISK 1¼ *cups* evaporated milk and pudding mix in medium bowl until well blended. Pour into crust.

MICROWAVE 2 cups marshmallows and *remaining ¼ cup* evaporated milk in medium, uncovered, microwave-safe bowl on HIGH (100%) power for 30 to 45 seconds; stir until smooth. Let stand for 15 minutes. Gently fold in whipped topping. Spoon marshmallow mixture over chocolate layer; smooth top with spatula.

REFRIGERATE for 2 hours or until set. Top with remaining 1 cup marshmallows and morsels.   *Makes 8 servings*

Tip: For a gooey S'more topping, place chilled pie on a baking sheet. Preheat broiler. Place baking sheet with pie on rack 6 inches from broiler unit (pie top should be at least 4 inches from broiler unit). Broil for 30 seconds or until marshmallows are light brown and morsels are shiny. Watch carefully as browning occurs very fast. A handheld kitchen butane torch can be used as well.

Old-Fashioned Chocolate Cream Pie

1 unbaked 9-inch pie crust
¾ cup sugar
½ cup unsweetened cocoa powder
¼ cup cornstarch
¼ teaspoon salt
3 cups milk, divided
1 egg, beaten
2 teaspoons vanilla
1 cup thawed whipped topping

1. Preheat oven to 400°F. Prick holes in bottom of crust with fork. Bake 10 minutes or until lightly browned. Cool 15 minutes on wire rack.

2. Combine sugar, cocoa, cornstarch and salt in medium saucepan. Slowly stir in milk and egg; let stand 5 minutes. Cook over medium heat 4 to 6 minutes or until mixture comes to a boil, stirring frequently. Boil 30 seconds, stirring constantly. Remove from heat. Cover surface of filling with plastic wrap to keep hot and prevent skin from forming. Cool to room temperature.

3. Spread filling in prepared crust. Cover and refrigerate at least 2 hours. Spread whipped topping over filling just before serving.

Makes 8 servings

Old-Fashioned Chocolate Cream Pie

Chocolate Magic Mousse Pie

1 envelope unflavored gelatin
2 tablespoons cold water
¼ cup boiling water
1 cup sugar
½ cup HERSHEY®S Cocoa
2 cups (1 pint) cold whipping cream
2 teaspoons vanilla extract
1 packaged (8-inch) graham cracker crumb crust (6 ounces)
   Refrigerated light whipped cream in pressurized can or frozen
      whipped topping, thawed
   HERSHEY®S MINI KISSES Brand Milk Chocolates

1. Sprinkle gelatin over cold water in small bowl; let stand 2 minutes to soften. Add boiling water; stir until gelatin is completely dissolved and mixture is clear. Cool slightly.

2. Mix sugar and cocoa in large bowl; add whipping cream and vanilla. Beat on medium speed, scraping bottom of bowl often, until mixture is stiff. Pour in gelatin mixture; beat until well blended.

3. Spoon into crust. Refrigerate about 3 hours. Garnish with whipped cream and chocolates. Cover; store leftover pie in refrigerator.

Makes 6 to 8 servings

Powdered gelatin will last indefinitely if it is wrapped airtight and stored in a cool, dry place. It is important to soak gelatin in cold liquid for several minutes (as the recipe directs) before dissolving it, so the gelatin granules soften, swell and dissolve smoothly when heated. When heated, gelatin mixtures should never be brought to a boil or the ability of the gelatin to set will be destroyed.

Chocolate Magic Mousse Pie

Mocha Decadence Pie

4 ounces semisweet chocolate
2 cups whipping cream, divided
½ cup plus 1 tablespoon sugar, divided
3 eggs
2 teaspoons instant coffee granules
1 teaspoon vanilla, divided
1 (6-ounce) graham cracker pie crust

1. Place chocolate in small microwavable bowl. Microwave on HIGH 1½ minutes or until melted, stirring after 1 minute.

2. Combine 1 cup cream and ½ cup sugar in medium saucepan over medium heat. Cook until sugar is dissolved, stirring constantly. Beat eggs in small bowl; stir in ¼ cup cream mixture. Pour egg mixture into cream mixture 4 to 5 minutes or until thickened, stirring constantly. Pour into large bowl. Beat in melted chocolate, coffee granules and ½ teaspoon vanilla with electric mixer at low speed. Beat at medium speed 2 minutes. Pour into crust. Cool 15 minutes. Cover and refrigerate 3 hours or overnight.

3. Beat remaining 1 cup cream in medium bowl with electric mixer at high speed 1 minute. Add remaining 1 tablespoon sugar and ½ teaspoon vanilla. Beat until soft peaks form. Top each slice with whipped cream.

Makes 8 servings

Mocha Decadence Pie

Upside-Down Hot Fudge Sundae Pie

⅔ cup butter or margarine
⅓ cup HERSHEY®S Cocoa
2 eggs
¼ cup milk
1 teaspoon vanilla extract
1 cup packed light brown sugar
½ cup granulated sugar
1 tablespoon all-purpose flour
⅛ teaspoon salt
1 unbaked 9-inch pie crust
2 bananas, peeled and thinly sliced
Ice cream, any flavor
Whipped topping

1. Heat oven to 350°F.

2. Melt butter in medium saucepan over low heat. Add cocoa; stir until smooth. Remove from heat. Stir together eggs, milk and vanilla in small bowl. Add egg mixture to cocoa mixture; stir with whisk until smooth and slightly thickened. Add brown sugar, granulated sugar, flour and salt; stir with whisk until smooth. Pour mixture into unbaked crust.

3. Bake 30 to 35 minutes until edge is set. (Center will be soft.) Cool about 2 hours. Just before serving, top each serving with banana slices, ice cream and whipped topping. *Makes 8 servings*

Upside-Down Hot Fudge Sundae Pie

Fruit-Filled Favorites

Fruit and Nut Chocolate Chip Pie

2 eggs
½ cup packed brown sugar
¼ cup granulated sugar
1 teaspoon vanilla
½ teaspoon grated orange peel
⅛ teaspoon salt
1 cup (2 sticks) unsalted butter, melted and cooled
½ cup all-purpose flour
1 cup semisweet chocolate chips
1 cup chopped pecans or walnuts
1 cup dried cranberries or raisins
1 unbaked 9-inch pie crust
Whipped cream (optional)

1. Preheat oven to 325°F.

2. Whisk eggs, brown sugar, granulated sugar, vanilla, orange peel and salt in large bowl. Whisk in butter and flour until blended. Stir in chocolate chips, pecans and cranberries. Spread evenly in crust.

3. Bake 50 minutes or until top is puffed and golden brown. Cool completely on wire rack. Serve with whipped cream, if desired.

Makes 8 servings

Prep Time: 10 minutes
Bake Time: 50 minutes

Blackberry Custard Pie

Single-Crust Pie Pastry (recipe follows)
½ cup sugar
3 tablespoons cornstarch
1¼ cups milk
1 tablespoon lemon juice
2 teaspoons grated lemon peel
2 eggs, lightly beaten
2 cups blackberries

1. Preheat oven to 425°F. Prepare Single-Crust Pie Pastry.

2. Pierce crust evenly with fork. Cut square of foil 4 inches larger than pie pan. Line crust with foil; fill with dried beans, uncooked rice or ceramic pie weights. Bake 10 minutes or until set. Remove foil lining and beans. Bake 5 minutes or until lightly browned. Cool completely on wire rack.

3. Combine sugar and cornstarch in small saucepan. Stir in milk, lemon juice and peel; cook and stir over medium heat until mixture boils and thickens. Boil 1 minute, stirring constantly. Stir ½ cup hot milk mixture into eggs; stir egg mixture back into saucepan. Cook over low heat until thickened, stirring constantly. Spoon into crust. Cool to room temperature; refrigerate 3 hours or until set. Arrange blackberries on custard. *Makes 8 servings*

Single-Crust Pie Pastry

1¼ cups all-purpose flour
¼ teaspoon baking powder
Dash salt
¼ cup canola or vegetable oil
3 tablespoons milk, divided

1. Combine flour, baking powder and salt in medium bowl. Add oil and 2 tablespoons milk; mix well. Add enough remaining milk to hold mixture together. Shape dough into ball.

2. Flatten dough to 1-inch thickness on 12-inch square of waxed paper; cover with second square of waxed paper. Roll out gently to form 12-inch round crust. Mend any tears or ragged edges by pressing together with fingers. *Do not moisten.* Remove one layer waxed paper from crust. Place dough, paper side up, in 9-inch pie pan. Peel off remaining paper. Press pastry into pan and flute edge. *Makes 1 pastry*

Blackberry Custard Pie

Tart Cherry Pie

Double-Crust Pie Pastry (page 200)
2 cans (about 14 ounces each) tart cherries, packed in juice
1½ cups granulated sugar
¼ cup quick-cooking tapioca
1 teaspoon ground cinnamon
1 teaspoon grated lemon peel
2 tablespoons unsalted butter, cut into small cubes
1 egg, beaten
1 teaspoon water
Coarse sugar

1. Prepare Double-Crust Pie Pastry.

2. Preheat oven to 425°F. Drain cherries, reserving ½ cup juice. Place cherries and reserved juice in large bowl. Combine granulated sugar, tapioca, cinnamon and lemon peel in small bowl. Add to cherries; mix well. Set aside.

3. Roll out one disc of pastry into 12-inch circle on lightly floured surface. Line 9-inch pie pan with pastry, allowing excess dough to hang over edge. Pour cherry mixture into crust; sprinkle evenly with butter.

4. Roll out remaining disc of pastry into 11-inch circle on lightly floured surface. Make slits in pastry with sharp knife. Top pie with second pastry. Fold edge under; seal and flute edge. Beat egg and water in small bowl. Brush top crust lightly with egg mixture; sprinkle with coarse sugar. Place pie on baking sheet.

5. Bake 15 minutes. *Reduce oven temperature to 350°F.* Bake 30 to 35 minutes or until crust is brown and juices are bubbly, covering loosely with foil during last 10 minutes of baking to prevent overbrowning. Cool on wire rack. Serve warm or at room temperature. *Makes 8 servings*

Tart Cherry Pie

Lattice Pineapple Pie

1 can (20 ounces) DOLE® Crushed Pineapple, undrained
½ cup sugar
2 tablespoons cornstarch
¼ teaspoon salt (optional)
1 tablespoon butter or margarine
1 tablespoon lemon juice
   Pastry for 9-inch double-crust pie

• Combine crushed pineapple, sugar, cornstarch and salt in saucepan. Cook, stirring, until thickened and clear. Stir in butter and lemon juice. Cool slightly.

• Pour filling into unbaked 9-inch pastry shell. Cut remaining pastry into 1-inch-wide strips for lattice top. Weave strips crisscross over pie to make lattice top. Pinch edges.

• Bake at 400°F 25 to 30 minutes or until lightly golden brown.

Makes 8 servings

Prep Time: 20 minutes
Bake Time: 30 minutes

Apple Raisin Pie

2 cans (20 ounces each) apple pie filling
1 cup raisins
½ teaspoon ground ginger, divided
1 unbaked 9-inch pie crust
¼ cup all-purpose flour
¼ cup packed brown sugar
2 tablespoons butter, melted
¾ cup chopped walnuts

1. Preheat oven to 375°F.

2. Combine pie filling, raisins and ¼ teaspoon ginger in large bowl; spoon into crust. Combine flour, sugar and remaining ¼ teaspoon ginger in small bowl; stir in butter until crumbly. Stir in walnuts; sprinkle over filling.

3. Bake 35 to 45 minutes or until topping is golden.   *Makes 8 servings*

Lattice Pineapple Pie

Raspberry Buttermilk Pie

1 unbaked deep-dish 9-inch pie crust
3 eggs
2 tablespoons all-purpose flour
1 cup buttermilk
¾ cup plus 2 tablespoons sugar
¼ cup (½ stick) unsalted butter, melted
¼ cup honey
½ teaspoon vanilla
¼ teaspoon salt
1½ cups fresh raspberries (do not substitute frozen)

1. Preheat oven to 425°F. Place crust on baking sheet. Bake 5 minutes. Remove from oven. Press down any areas that puff up. *Reduce oven temperature to 350°F.*

2. Beat eggs and flour in large bowl until blended. Beat in buttermilk, sugar, butter, honey, vanilla and salt until sugar is dissolved. Gently stir in raspberries. Pour into crust.

3. Bake 50 minutes or until knife inserted near center comes out clean. Let stand 30 minutes before slicing. *Makes 12 servings*

Fresh milk can be soured and used as a substitute for buttermilk. If a recipe calls for 1 cup of buttermilk, place 1 tablespoon lemon juice or distilled white vinegar in a measuring cup and add enough milk to measure 1 cup. Stir and let the mixture stand at room temperature 5 minutes.

Raspberry Buttermilk Pie

Deep-Dish Blueberry Pie

Double-Crust Pie Pastry (page 200)
6 cups fresh blueberries *or* 2 packages (16 ounces each) frozen
   blueberries, thawed and drained
2 tablespoons lemon juice
1¼ cups sugar
3 tablespoons quick-cooking tapioca
¼ teaspoon ground cinnamon
1 tablespoon butter, cubed

1. Prepare Double-Crust Pie Pastry. Preheat oven to 400°F.

2. Place blueberries in large bowl and sprinkle with lemon juice. Combine sugar, tapioca and cinnamon in small bowl; gently stir into blueberries until blended.

3. Roll one disc of dough into 12-inch circle on lightly floured surface. Line 9-inch deep-dish pie pan with pastry. Trim all but ½ inch of overhang. Pour blueberry mixture into pan; dot with butter.

4. Roll remaining disc of dough into 10-inch circle on lightly floured surface. Cut 4 or 5 shapes from dough for vents, using small cookie cutter or knife. Lift and center dough over blueberry mixture in pie pan. Trim dough, leaving 1-inch border. Fold excess dough under and even with pan edge; seal and flute edge.

5. Bake 15 minutes. *Reduce oven temperature to 350°F.* Bake 40 minutes or until crust is golden brown. Cool on wire rack 30 minutes before serving.   *Makes 12 servings*

Deep-Dish Blueberry Pie

Creamy Vanilla Apple Pie

1 egg
6 to 8 apples, peeled and sliced ¼ inch thick
1 cup sugar
1 cup vanilla yogurt
4 to 6 tablespoons all-purpose flour
1 teaspoon vanilla
½ teaspoon ground cinnamon
1 unbaked 9-inch pie crust
    Spicy Crumb Topping (recipe follows)

1. Preheat oven to 350°F.

2. Beat egg in medium bowl. Add apples, 1 cup sugar, yogurt, flour, vanilla and cinnamon; toss to coat. Transfer to crust.

3. Prepare Spicy Crumb Topping. Sprinkle over apple mixture.

4. Bake 1 hour or until topping is golden brown. Cool completely on wire rack.   *Makes 8 servings*

Spicy Crumb Topping

1 cup all-purpose flour
½ cup granulated sugar
½ cup packed brown sugar
½ cup (1 stick) butter, melted
¼ teaspoon ground cinnamon

Combine flour, ½ cup granulated sugar, brown sugar, butter and cinnamon in medium bowl; stir until blended.   *Makes about 2 cups*

Creamy Vanilla Apple Pie

Enlightened Fresh Triple-Berry Pie

1 unbaked 9-inch pie crust
1 lemon
4 cups fresh strawberries, stemmed and quartered, divided
½ cup sugar
½ cup water
2 tablespoons cornstarch
1 cup fresh blueberries
1 cup fresh raspberries
½ teaspoon vanilla or almond extract

1. Preheat oven to 475°F. Prick holes in bottom and side of crust with fork. Bake 12 minutes or until light brown. Place on wire rack. Finely grate lemon peel over crust; cool completely.

2. Combine 1 cup strawberries, sugar, water and cornstarch in food processor or blender; process until smooth. Transfer to medium saucepan; bring to a boil over medium-high heat. Boil 1 minute, stirring constantly. Remove from heat. Let stand 10 to 15 minutes to cool slightly.

3. Add remaining 3 cups strawberries, blueberries, raspberries and vanilla to strawberry mixture; stir gently. Spoon into crust. Cover with plastic wrap. Refrigerate until firm.   *Makes 8 servings*

Common thickeners for fruit pies are cornstarch, tapioca and flour. Cornstarch and tapioca create a translucent filling, while flour gives the filling a more opaque appearance.

Glazed Fresh Strawberry Pie

Cookie Crust
   1½ cups crushed shortbread cookies
   ⅓ cup butter, melted
   ¼ cup chopped almonds

Filling
   2 pints (about 2 pounds) strawberries, hulled
   ⅓ cup water
   1 cup sugar
   2 tablespoons ARGO® Corn Starch
   ½ teaspoon almond extract
   ¼ teaspoon salt
      Whipped topping (optional)

To Make Cookie Crust:
MIX all crust ingredients. Press into 9-inch pie pan. Bake at 350°F for 8 minutes or until lightly browned.

To Make Filling:
MASH (or purée) enough strawberries to equal 1 cup; add water. Combine sugar and corn starch in small saucepan. Stir in mashed strawberries.

COOK over medium heat, stirring constantly until mixture thickens and comes to a full boil (15 to 20 minutes). Boil 1 minute; remove from heat. Stir in almond extract and salt. Cool 10 minutes.

FILL cooled crust with remaining whole strawberries; pour cooked strawberry mixture over berries. Refrigerate at least 3 hours. Garnish with whipped topping, if desired. *Makes 8 servings*

Note: A baked 9-inch pie crust may be substituted for the cookie crust.

Prep Time: 30 minutes
Bake Time: 8 minutes
Cook Time: 15 to 20 minutes
Cool Time: 10 minutes
Chill Time: 3 hours

Peach Raspberry Pie

Single-Crust Pie Pastry (page 264)
Almond Crumb Topping (recipe follows)
5 cups peach slices (about 2 pounds)
2 tablespoons lemon juice
1 cup raspberries
½ cup granulated sugar
2 tablespoons quick-cooking tapioca
½ teaspoon ground cinnamon
¼ teaspoon ground nutmeg
Whipped cream (optional)

1. Prepare Single-Crust Pie Pastry. Prepare Almond Crumb Topping.

2. Preheat oven to 400°F. Roll out pastry into 11-inch circle on lightly floured surface. Line 9-inch pie plate with pastry; flute edge. Refrigerate 15 minutes.

3. Place peaches in large bowl. Sprinkle with lemon juice; toss to coat. Stir in raspberries. Combine granulated sugar, tapioca, cinnamon and nutmeg in small bowl. Sprinkle over fruit mixture; toss to coat. Spread evenly in crust. Sprinkle with Almond Crumb Topping.

4. Bake 15 minutes. *Reduce oven temperature to 350°F.* Bake 30 minutes or until bubbly. Cool 15 minutes on wire rack. Serve with whipped cream, if desired. *Makes 8 servings*

Almond Crumb Topping

⅔ cup old-fashioned or quick oats
¼ cup all-purpose flour
¼ cup slivered almonds
¼ cup packed brown sugar
½ teaspoon ground cinnamon
3 tablespoons unsalted butter, softened

Combine oats, flour, almonds, brown sugar and cinnamon in medium bowl. Blend in butter until mixture resembles coarse crumbs.
Makes about 1½ cups

Peach Raspberry Pie

Acknowledgments

The publisher would like to thank the companies and organizations listed below for the use of their recipes and photographs in this publication.

ACH Food Companies, Inc.

Del Monte Foods

Dole Food Company, Inc.

The Hershey Company

®, TM, © 2010 Kellogg NA Co.

Kraft Foods Global, Inc.

National Honey Board

Nestlé USA

Northwest Cherry Growers

Ortega®, A Division of B&G Foods, Inc.

Reckitt Benckiser LLC.

Riviana Foods Inc.

Sargento® Foods Inc.

Tyson Foods, Inc.

Unilever

USA Rice Federation®

US Dry Bean Council

Veg•All®

Watkins Incorporated

Wisconsin Milk Marketing Board

VOLUME MEASUREMENTS (dry)

$^1/_8$ teaspoon = 0.5 mL
$^1/_4$ teaspoon = 1 mL
$^1/_2$ teaspoon = 2 mL
$^3/_4$ teaspoon = 4 mL
1 teaspoon = 5 mL
1 tablespoon = 15 mL
2 tablespoons = 30 mL
$^1/_4$ cup = 60 mL
$^1/_3$ cup = 75 mL
$^1/_2$ cup = 125 mL
$^2/_3$ cup = 150 mL
$^3/_4$ cup = 175 mL
1 cup = 250 mL
2 cups = 1 pint = 500 mL
3 cups = 750 mL
4 cups = 1 quart = 1 L

VOLUME MEASUREMENTS (fluid)

1 fluid ounce (2 tablespoons) = 30 mL
4 fluid ounces ($^1/_2$ cup) = 125 mL
8 fluid ounces (1 cup) = 250 mL
12 fluid ounces (1$^1/_2$ cups) = 375 mL
16 fluid ounces (2 cups) = 500 mL

WEIGHTS (mass)

$^1/_2$ ounce = 15 g
1 ounce = 30 g
3 ounces = 90 g
4 ounces = 120 g
8 ounces = 225 g
10 ounces = 285 g
12 ounces = 360 g
16 ounces = 1 pound = 450 g

DIMENSIONS

$^1/_{16}$ inch = 2 mm
$^1/_8$ inch = 3 mm
$^1/_4$ inch = 6 mm
$^1/_2$ inch = 1.5 cm
$^3/_4$ inch = 2 cm
1 inch = 2.5 cm

OVEN TEMPERATURES

250°F = 120°C
275°F = 140°C
300°F = 150°C
325°F = 160°C
350°F = 180°C
375°F = 190°C
400°F = 200°C
425°F = 220°C
450°F = 230°C

BAKING PAN SIZES

Utensil	Size in Inches/Quarts	Metric Volume	Size in Centimeters
Baking or Cake Pan (square or rectangular)	$8 \times 8 \times 2$	2 L	$20 \times 20 \times 5$
	$9 \times 9 \times 2$	2.5 L	$23 \times 23 \times 5$
	$12 \times 8 \times 2$	3 L	$30 \times 20 \times 5$
	$13 \times 9 \times 2$	3.5 L	$33 \times 23 \times 5$
Loaf Pan	$8 \times 4 \times 3$	1.5 L	$20 \times 10 \times 7$
	$9 \times 5 \times 3$	2 L	$23 \times 13 \times 7$
Round Layer Cake Pan	$8 \times 1^1/_2$	1.2 L	20×4
	$9 \times 1^1/_2$	1.5 L	23×4
Pie Plate	$8 \times 1^1/_4$	750 mL	20×3
	$9 \times 1^1/_4$	1 L	23×3
Baking Dish or Casserole	1 quart	1 L	—
	1$^1/_2$ quart	1.5 L	—
	2 quart	2 L	—